George Blenkhorn visits Bluenose II at Spessard Holland terminal Thursday — Tribune Photo by Gary Rings

BLUENOSE,
QUEEN of the
GRAND BANKS

CHILTON BOOK COMPANY
Philadelphia   New York   London

BLUENOSE, QUEEN of the GRAND BANKS

by Feenie Ziner

Illustrations, Zeke Ziner

For my mother, SOPHIE GUTTMAN KATZ,
who has always lived
within breathing distance of the sea

Acknowledgments

My warm and grateful thanks go to Mr. Don Oland, who, representing the entire Oland family, extended the invitation to my husband and myself to sail aboard *Bluenose II* when she departed from Expo '67 after playing host for the government of Canada throughout that great international exposition. It was an unforgettable five-day journey down the St. Lawrence River, through the Gulf of St. Lawrence, the Northumberland Strait, and around to Halifax, and Capt. Ellsworth T. Coggins made it seem a whole lot safer than it really was.

Wallace Zinck, crew member of *Bluenose II*, has been as tireless a researcher as he is an intrepid sailor. I am deeply indebted to him for help and friendship.

Brian Backman, co-author of *Bluenose,* has been an indispensable source of information and encouragement. His extraordinary gifts as a storyteller invested the facts with magic and brought the *Bluenose* story to life for me.

Thomas Radall, who has been called "Nova Scotia's writer-in-residence," drew upon his prodigious knowledge of Nova Scotian history to send me detailed information about the history of Lunenburg just for the asking. James Kinley and Jack Pardy, both of Lunenburg, spent hours sharing with me their personal experiences with *Bluenose*.

To Doris and Irvin Block of Sea Cliff, Long Island, I owe my first glimmering of the joys and perils of sailing. It was aboard the good ship *Tzatzka* that I first learned the meaning of "ready about," felt the terror of a broken mast, and fully appreciated the pride of an accomplished skipper in his craft.

My family has been good-humored and patient during the production of this book—especially my husband, Zeke. He nursed me through the only attack of seasickness I ever suffered —for a solid week when, tucked into my very own bed, I dreamed of our forthcoming voyage aboard the beautiful *Bluenose II*.

F.Z.

Montreal, Canada

BLUENOSE,
QUEEN of the
GRAND BANKS

Chapter One

There are several explanations of the name "Bluenose" to be found in books, but the only one which makes unmistakably good sense to the newcomer to the Canadian province of Nova Scotia has to do with the weather. Nova Scotians will tell you with pride that their weather is so invigorating, so good for the health that people in Nova Scotia live longer than they do any-where else on the North American continent. They will boast of their weather even as the fog rolls in in a thick wet blanket from the North Atlantic or the wind sings up and down the scale. "Oh, my," says the loyal Nova Scotian, "I just couldn't stand the heat down south. I suppose it's all right for those soft-living Yankees. . . ."

If he knows you well, he will tell you much more about "the Americans," which in Nova Scotia mostly means the fishermen of Gloucester, Massachusetts, with perhaps Boston, New York, and Washington thrown in for good measure. Not much of what he will say will be complimentary, for Nova Scotians have been trading insults with their Yankee neighbors for nearly three hundred years, and neither side has ever run out of unpleasant things to say. While he talks, the Nova Scotian's cheeks get redder, his eyebrows gather frost, and his nose turns a delicate blue. This color scheme does not make him an American by any means.

"I'm a Bluenose!" he proclaims with a cheerful chattering of his teeth.

The story we are about to tell concerns the building and sailing of the fastest fishing schooner ever built—a big, beautiful, blue-black vessel called *Bluenose,* and from her name you may guess she represented all of Nova Scotia. In a way she also represented all of Canada, for she was as dear to the hearts of the people of Medicine Hat, Alberta, as to the people of her own rocky, sea-rimmed province.

Bluenose became the Queen of the Grand Banks in a series of races called "The Halifax Herald North Atlantic Fisherman's International Competition," held between 1920 and 1938 just outside the two harbors of Halifax, Nova Scotia and Gloucester, Massachusetts. Five times in her long lifetime she defeated the best vessels her American competitors could build. The honors heaped upon her would have turned any human head. In 1933 *Bluenose* represented Canada at the Chicago world's fair, sailing all the way up the St. Lawrence River and through the Great Lakes long before that route was opened to oceangoing travel by the completion of the St. Lawrence Seaway.

Bluenose was the only sailing ship present when King George V and Queen Mary of England celebrated their silver jubilee in 1935. She was a standout among the hundred-odd naval vessels drawn up for royal review off Spithead, England. A hardworking fishing boat, scraped of her muck and fish slime, she was as tidy for that occasion as the smartest ship of the Royal Navy. King George entertained her skipper, the famed Capt. Angus Walters, aboard the royal yacht, and Walters found the kind to be "a wery nice, ordinary kind o' feller."

Bluenose was honored by one of the most beautifully engraved postage stamps ever produced in Canada, and since 1937 her handsome profile has shared the surface of the Canadian ten-cent piece with the profile of another monarch, Queen Elizabeth II of England.

More astonishing than all the official honors, however, is a story told by a Canadian film-maker who was traveling through northern Mexico, more than twenty years after *Bluenose* lay broken-backed and far from home on the floor of the Atlantic Ocean. The Mexican country-side was stark and primitive, and the traveler stopped at a woodcutter's hut to ask directions. On the thatched wall of the woodcutter's workshop hung a half-hull model of a wooden sailing ship. The spoon-bowed profile, the uptilted bowsprit, the slight tumble home of her hull were unmistakable to his Nova Scotian eye. He was certain that the ship model had come to this place by some strange and outlandish accident, and that her identity was completely unknown. "Do you know the name of that vessel?" he asked the Mexican. "Of course," the woodcutter replied. "That was the fastest sailing vessel ever built. She was called *Bluenose*."

Many other vessels have won races in their day without earning for themselves the deep affection which people the world over have felt for *Bluenose,* and only part of that feeling can be explained. She was beautiful, and people loved her for that. Without understanding a single element of the shipbuilder's craft or a single point of sailing, a man could forget himself, be lifted out of his everyday world by the sight of her, and maybe it was that moment of forgetting that he remembered best.

But for her mast, she was Canadian through and through. Designed by a Canadian, built by Canadians, constructed of Canadian wood and canvas, she sailed to victory with a Canadian skipper and a Canadian crew. And she beat her big, rich, next-door neighbor.

Large as Canada is, it has one tenth the population of the United States and far fewer developed resources. Canadians hate the role of poor relative, and they are forever being put in that position; for whatever Canada does, the United States does more of it, does it faster, and often does it better. With the building of *Bluenose* the tables were turned. Canada had produced a champion, and Americans did not like to acknowledge it. Down in Gloucester, Massachusetts, they are still saying that *Bluenose* didn't really win. But no doubt exists in the minds of Canadians on that score. For them, the victories of *Bluenose* were like the victory of a David over a Goliath.

It is time that Americans, too, understood the story of *Bluenose*. She came into being because of the border which

3

separates the United States and Canada, and was a direct product of the rivalry between the two countries. But the drama of her life has meaning far beyond the narrow prejudice of national boundaries. *Bluenose* was built by men who loved their craft enough to make of her a work of art, and in that sense their achievement belongs equally to everyone in the world who has a job and wants to do it well. She was not just the plaything of some millionaire sportsman. She earned her keep in one of the toughest and most dangerous of trades. Her daily life involved hardship and drudgery. There is no glamour in fish slime, no sportsmanship in a race for bait, no glory in working for six weeks in the fiercest weather and fetching up in home port with six dollars in your pocket for your pains. This was the life *Bluenose* shared with hundreds of other "saltbankers" and, to some extent, with fishermen everywhere and in every time. She represented not only beauty, speed, and love of craft; she represented those indispensable ingredients of all great lives—hard work, modesty, and endurance.

Capt. Wilson Berringer was Skipper of Bluenose when she was lost on Haiti. There was ugly talk about Insurance playing a part in her loss.

Chapter Two

To most of us, anything which has to do with sail-powered vessels is automatically tucked into the mental slot reserved for the nineteenth century. We think of clipper ships rounding the Horn in the teeth of a gale, or of full-blown square-riggers bearing down upon a palm jungle island as dark-skinned men in long canoes skim out to greet them.

It comes as something of a shock to realize that some sailing vessels continued to live a rather lusty life along the northeast coast of the United States and Canada well into the twentieth century and that the most perfect examples of the boatbuilders' craft were not even created until after World War I.

The fact is that *Bluenose* lived her entire life between two world wars. If a tombstone had been erected over her grave on the old Spanish Main, it would have read, "Here lies *Bluenose*, born a queen in Lunenburg, Nova Scotia, March 26, 1921. Died a derelict off Haiti, January 28, 1946."

The story of the life of *Bluenose* is a downhill tale, all except for its very ending. Her beginnings were undertaken in an atmosphere of glory and expectation, like the birth of a last and long-awaited child into a family in which all the other children had long since grown up and moved away. Her end was as sad as death itself—but for the odd and ironic twist which brought her back to life long after her ghost had become as familiar a fixture in Nova Scotia as a teakettle on a stove.

She came into existence at a time when everyone really knew that the days of sail and canvas were numbered. *Bluenose* and her fellow saltbankers out of Lunenburg and Gloucester were carry-overs from a passing era. They reached the peak of their perfection and performance in a kind of Indian summer, when competition from steam-powered iron vessels had already made them uneconomical investments. The steam-powered fishing boat which made its first appearance off the coast of Nova Scotia around the time of World War I was stronger, faster, and larger than the wooden vessels it eventually replaced. Iron boats had a bigger carrying capacity and could employ much heavier fishing equipment than any sail-driven ship. But though they were safer and more comfortable than the old-style sailing schooners, most fishermen hated them thoroughly and fought their coming with all the strength and determination at their command. Until 1965 Nova Scotia, which for a time held the world's record as a builder of fishing vessels, had still not built its first steel trawler.

While technologically and historically *Bluenose* was obsolete before the first plank was cut to brace her keel, the hope, the pride, and the striving for excellence which went into the building of her were as enduring as the human impulse which put men upon the surface of the moon.

⚓

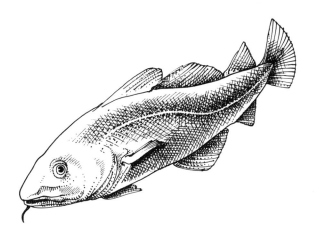

In order to understand the story of *Bluenose* we have to understand something about the fishing industry in which she served. Specifically she was built to fish on the Grand Banks for salt cod. She was a dory fisherman, an eight-sailed schooner carrying a crew of twenty-one men.

Outside of Nova Scotia, Newfoundland or Gloucester, Massachusetts, it is unlikely that you will ever see whole dry salt cod, though they are sold by the thousands in the wharfside marketplaces of Brazil, Portugal, and the West Indies. But for three centuries—roughly between 1630 and 1930—there was not a single village along the North Atlantic coast from Cape Cod to Newfoundland which did not have a section known as the "flakes."

The flakes were not only *on* the fringe of the town; they *were* the fringe of the town—a grayish white ruffle skirting the sea rim. Flakes were acres of wooden racks, waist-high to a man, upon which the split halves of codfish were laid to dry in the sun and the wind. For the occasional visitor to the northeast coast, the gray-white flakes made a pleasant color variation along the grass-green shore. When the wind blew in from the sea toward the land, the flakes might even have looked from a distance like a field of daisies. But when the wind shifted and blew over the land toward the sea, the odor of drying fish was heavy enough to sink a dory!

The reason for the catching and drying of all that fish was not because fishermen and their families chose an all-fish diet. Not for nothing are dwellers by the shore called "herring chokers." The reason for the flakes and the fishermen who kept them filled with salt cod was that before the invention of artificial refrigeration, dried and salted cod was one of the very few protein foods in the world which could be preserved almost indefinitely, even in a hot, moist climate. The keeping power of well-dried salt cod made it possible for men to make long voyages to distant places. Salt cod nourished the populations of France, Spain, Portugal, and Italy for centuries, and later fed whole populations in Central and South America.

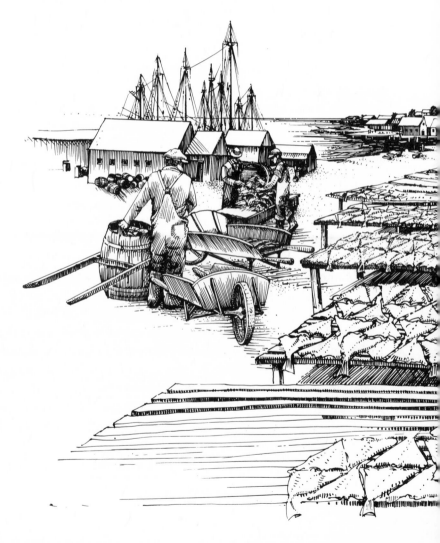

The richest cod-fishing grounds in the world lay for centuries between 100 and 200 miles east of Nova Scotia and 50 to 100 miles south of Newfoundland. This area of the Atlantic Ocean is known as the Grand Banks (see page 109), and while it is roughly bounded by Canadian territory, its waters are international. The Grand Banks themselves are a group of fifteen underwater islands, formed in millennia past by deposits from the Gulf Stream moving northward and the Labrador current moving south. The Banks were first discovered by Portuguese and Basque fishermen long before Columbus, and fishermen have been going there continuously since the early 1400s. Indeed, one of the most important reasons that the French and the

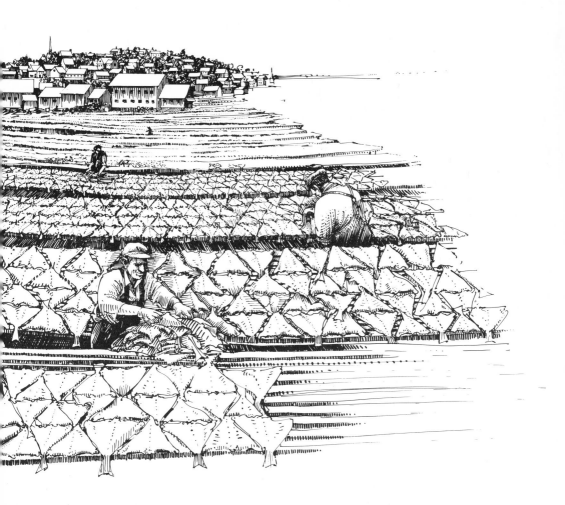

English began to settle on the northeast coast of America was in order to be able to dry their catch of cod ashore on very much the same sort of flakes that were still in use in the first half of the twentieth century.

It is very hard to conceive of the quantity of fish that has been caught on the Banks. Nowadays a hundred thousand fishermen from many countries take their catch from the Grand Banks each year. In the first two decades of the twentieth century, just before (the) *Bluenose* was built, 1,100,000,000 pounds of cod a year were caught on the Banks, and in some years after that, the catch has been even greater.

But what does 1,100,000,000 pounds of *anything* really mean? We could try to estimate how many people could have a single meal from such a catch, or how many countries could feed their population for a year on it, but it would still not tell us very much. One billion, one hundred million is a good many digits on a calculating machine or a printed page, but 1,100,000,000 pounds of wet, cold, slippery, scaly fish gathered one hook at a time from a savage sea from the surface of an invisible island and carried to shore by a fleet of small wooden vessels manned by a few thousand men . . . well, that represents a kind of miracle.

To produce and reproduce this miracle year in and year out, men needed a tremendous store of knowledge and experience; they needed extraordinary strength and courage; and they needed the best and most dependable techniques and equipment that could possibly be devised. Nova Scotia also had the wood from which fishing vessels could be built, so the construction of a fleet of great sailing boats was an important enough activity to occupy a great part of the population of the province.

The manning of those vessels was just as important as the building of them, and here Nova Scotia contributed an enormous share as well. Fishing was not a job a man took by walking into an employment office and putting his name down on a printed form. Fishing was a craft he inherited from his father, his uncles, his grandfather, his next-door neighbor. By the age of five, a boy learned to jump out of bed and look out at the weather before he even looked down at his feet. He lived his life to the sounds of wind and wood and water. Fishing was his style,

his reason for existence, the ruler by which he measured his achievements as a man. Fishermen were, and in a way remain, a race apart—poor, proud, and possessed of a mysterious link with the source of all life. As they say in Lunenburg, "The sea got in your blood."

From the beginning of its recorded history and probably for a long time before that, the fishing industry played an exceedingly important part in Canada's prosperity. While the total supply of fish on the Grand Banks is still stupendous, it seems to have decreased sharply in the past fifty years. The fishing industry as a whole is nearly as subject to change and chance as the single fellow who goes out with his fishing pole and lunch basket to try his luck. If the season's catch is very good and the supply of fish is large, prices usually drop, and the fisherman's wage drops with it. If the catch is poor and supply is short, the market can disappear altogether. Furthermore, people's tastes in food change. In the United States and Canada, inland people are only beginning to learn to incorporate fish into their diets as freezing and fast shipping have made fresh-tasting fish a supermarket staple.

In countries where money is scarce, the economy is likely to be unstable too, and people may not have cash to pay for food that has been imported from great distances, even if the price is very cheap. Right now the supply of salt cod is greater than the demand. But with the rise in the world's population, a product like ground fish meal could become as important as wheat or rice in the world's diet.

Each shift in the way the fish catch is bought or processed or distributed requires elaborate changes in the methods used to catch the fish and carry it to market. Salt cod requires an entirely different apparatus from fresh or frozen cod. Changes from one style to another were and are expensive to make. While today some of the Banks are "as crowded as downtown on a Saturday night," at the time *Bluenose* was built, fishing was still being done on a small scale by a few skilled men working over an area of several hundred square miles. Changes in the styles of fishing boats were made more easily in the United States than they have been in Canada—for reasons we shall come to later. But the basic

12

[handwritten margin note:] The supply of fish on the Banks is rapidly dwindling owing to being fished so heavily by modern factory ships that scoop up everything in the way of fish, small & large.

problems of the fishing industry in the United States and Canada, or more specifically the Gloucester fleet and the Lunenburg fleet, have been similar if not the same. These problems have shaped the thoughts, the feelings, and the traditions of the men who have struggled with them. The sea which mothered them all cast them into the mold of brothers, brothers who understand and compete with each other precisely because they are so much alike.

This, then, was why, when Nova Scotians issued the challenge for the building of vessels for an international fishing-schooner race, they issued the challenge to the Gloucestermen, and to no other. The Gloucester fleet was also caught in the squeeze of history. For them as well, the day of the wooden fishing schooner was past and the handwriting on the wall could be read in any language. No one knew better than the fisherman himself that once he had landed his fish safely at the dock he had overcome only the first of many perils. The transaction at the weighing scale and the cashier's desk could undo in a second what all his brain and muscle and courage had accomplished at sea. But so long as men are men, they will continue to do things which reason tells them are neither practical nor profitable. The fishing men who sailed those ships were the bearers of a great tradition. In spite of all the statistics and charts and predictions and public speeches that said, "You are impractical, foolhardy, obsolete, doomed," they put everything they had into the building of a fleet of superb wooden vessels, and went on to sail them and fish in them and go down with them, too, when the time came.

Perhaps it was Capt. Angus Walters, the tough and wiry little skipper of *Bluenose,* who came closest to explaining the building of nineteenth-century vessels in the twentieth century. "I never wanted to be better than any other man," he once said. "I always wanted to be just as good." As the captain of *Bluenose,* he certainly fulfilled that goal. But the remarkable thing about it was that in doing so, he made other men, too, proud of the fact that they were men.

Chapter Three

Let us go to Halifax, Nova Scotia, in the year 1919, to a musty, old-fashioned building a few blocks uphill from the docks, for it was there that the Fishermen's International Competition began. It was the office of the editor and publisher of the *Halifax Herald and Mail,* the city's largest daily newspaper. The name neatly lettered on the frosted-glass door was that of Senator William B. Dennis—"Senator" because he served as a representative in Nova Scotia's Parliament. The man who sat behind that big paper-strewn desk was clearly a man of energy and influence in his province.

Senator Dennis's newspaper was a very lively journal, as it needed to be at a time when it looked as if the world were turning on its head. The columns of the paper were black with startling headlines. Revolutions and insurrections were wiping out one European government after another. South of Nova Scotia, in the turbulent United States, there were race riots and strikes. The spirit of Bolshevism even penetrated staid old Nova Scotia, whose many thousands of coal miners in organized trade unions called for an end to private profit and for the establishment of a workers' democracy. All up and down the east coast of the United States, fishermen were on strike, demanding a living wage, an eight-hour day, and a union shop. People whose lives had been torn by the recently ended war were wondering what the world was coming to.

Dennis was the sort of newspaperman who not only reported the news, he believed in making some of it himself. He began a campaign to buy a car for the use of wounded war veterans who were hospitalized in Halifax. He called for the immediate planning of an airport in Halifax, though the very first crossing of the Atlantic Ocean by a lighter-than-air dirigible was a scarcely accomplished fact. Proudly he published a photo of the signing of the Treaty of Versailles, carried from Edinburgh, Scotland, to Roosevelt Field, Long Island, in the mail pouch of the dirigible R-34 at an average speed of 50 m.p.h. and delivered to his desk in the record-breaking time of thirteen days. Underneath the photo were an advertisement offering tooth extractions at twenty-five cents apiece, and a column of advice to young ladies whose mothers were daring enough to invite an eligible suitor to tea.

But Senator Dennis paid attention to the dull news on the inside pages as well: financial reports, legal news, and—most of all—shipping, shipbuilding, and fishing news, for these were the cold sober facts on which the future of the province depended. A third of Nova Scotia's wooden ships had been sunk by German submarines during the war, and the need for transport was urgent. The fishing industry was trying to stagger to its feet after severe losses of men, and markets. Foreign currencies were changing faster than a man could calculate; inflation was wiping out whole economies, and the price of salt cod had dropped below ten cents a pound. The old-time schoonermen were worried. Nearly half the vessels clearing port in Halifax were steam-powered now. Even though the yards from Digby to Yarmouth were launching an average of one tern schooner every three days, some feared the building boom would be followed by a bust.

An assistant brought Senator Dennis his weekly packet of papers shipped up from New York, and Dennis turned to the sport pages for relief. "The New York Yacht Club," he read, "has announced postponement of the race scheduled for today because of a twenty-three-mile-an-hour gale." His laughter could be heard all the way down to the pressroom. "Twenty-three miles an hour! Why, *our* fishermen down in Lunenburg would wonder if it was worth their while to hoist sail in a light breeze like that!" The joke went round the table at lunch where H. R. Sil-

15

ver, Reg Corbett, and Harry de Wolf, all of them businessmen in Halifax, met with their friend Senator Dennis.

"Remember when the America's Cup Races began, back in 1851? Those blasted Yankees built a yacht with such a shallow draft that she sailed right along the shore and trimmed nine miles off the racing course. She won the cup all right, but do you call that fair play? Sportsmanship? Why, it was just a lowdown Yankee trick!" said one of the men. The seventy-year-old story went round and round the table, as savory a morsel for the proud Canadians as Senator Dennis's fresh tidbit from the New York Yacht Club.

"Why don't we give our men down in Lunenburg a chance to show their heels to those lily-livered millionaires down there? Let's have a real competition . . . against the Gloucester boys . . . real sailors, real fishermen! We'll show them how to handle a boat in a fair breeze o' wind!" spoke up another.

And that, approximately, was how the Fishermen's International Competition began.

Halifax men went down to Lunenburg and talked it over with some of the skippers of the saltbank fleet. They found them willing—eager, even. The Haligonians formed themselves into a committee and raised $4000 as a cash prize. They ordered the casting of a four-foot silver loving cup as a trophy. Their Gloucester business friends formed a sponsoring committee of their own, composed of shipowners and fish dealers as well as ship designers. The rules of the competition were drawn up with care. Its official title was "The Halifax Herald North Atlantic Fishermen's International Competition," and the trustees included the Premier of Nova Scotia, the Mayor of Halifax, and William Roue, later to be the designer of *Bluenose*.

While it was called an international race, it did not include the French-speaking Nova Scotians of the "French"—or "Fundy"—Shore, most of whom were involved in the inshore and fresh fisheries; nor did it include the Portuguese, who fished on the Banks for six months at a time and returned to Portugal without landing or drying their catches in Canada. Portuguese vessels, with a good local supply of salt at their disposal, salted down the fish heavily as they caught them, and their methods

16

had not changed greatly in the five hundred years they had been coming to the Banks. Their vessels were not built for speed but for carrying capacity, and their contacts with the Nova Scotians were distant, if not hostile. There were virtually no Portuguese immigrants living on Nova Scotian soil, though Portuguese did settle in great numbers in the Cape Cod and Gloucester areas. They worked on American vessels, and if they took part in the races at all, it was just as they fished—as American citizens rather than as Portuguese.

To qualify for the races, a vessel had to be a saltbanker with at least one season of work on the Grand Banks under her belt. This ruling eliminated a large number of American contenders, for most of the American fleet had become "fresh" fishermen, packing their catch in ice and speeding with it back to market. The gear for fresh-fishing was considerably ligher than for the salt-fish industry. Most of the American vessels made ten-day trips rather than the six-week-to-two-month trips made by the Nova Scotians, who carried salt to partially preserve the catch before it was dried ashore. But there were still enough salt fishermen down in Gloucester to pick up the Canadian challenge, and they did it with a will.

It was still a small world out on the Banks, and most of the men knew one another well. In fact, many Gloucester skippers had been born in Newfoundland or Nova Scotia and were Yankees by transplantation. Every time the "Novies" met the "Yanks," they gave each other a "hook" (a challenge to race), and both groups welcomed the idea of a formal race to decide —officially and for all time—which nation built the better vessels.

There was much excitement down in Lunenburg when word got around that an international schooner race was in the making. Lunenburg, seventy miles south of Halifax, was the home of the greatest deep-sea-fishing fleet in the world. As a small town with a highly skilled and highly specialized population, Lunenburg, Nova Scotia, bore much the same relationship to her big-city sister, Halifax, that the town of Gloucester bore to the city of Boston. Halifax and Boston were both centers of trade and finance. Lunenburg and Gloucester were the two

17

great ports from which the fisheries were conducted, the places where the actual work was done.

Just as the Halifax businessmen, with their pride in Nova Scotia, had had a laugh on the New York Yacht Club, now the skippers of Lunenburg had a snort for the Halifax businessmen. For when the *Halifax Herald* published details of the contest rules, the skippers discovered that a time limit of nine hours had been set for the racing course. The course off Halifax harbor, where the first race was to be held, involved four turning points: Inner Automatic Buoy, Sambro Lightship, Outer Automatic Buoy, and Shut In Island Buoy, a total distance of thirty-nine nautical miles. "If a wessel couldn't sail that course in five hours, she's no business bein' in de race at all!" exclaimed the working fishermen. "Bunch o' paunchy old businessmen up there in Halifax, don't know nothin' about sailin'!" *right*

As it turned out, this was only the first of many sour observations—from both sides of the border—which would be made about the self-appointed committees who held the purses and made the decisions. As sharp as the conflict may have been between the Nova Scotians and the Yankees, it was never so sharp as that which eventually developed between the men who organized and financed the races and the men who actually did the sailing. But more of that later.

The first races were held at the end of the fishing season in October, 1920. Two series of trials were held, one in Gloucester and one in Halifax, to choose the contenders for the international trophy. Many bets were laid on Angus Walters, owner and skipper of the *Gilbert B. Walters,* for Angus was know all over the Banks as a master skipper and a highliner as well. The previous season, he had brought home a fare of 790,000 pounds of fish, enough to pay for his vessel two-and-a-half times over in a single season. Besides being a champion fish killer, Angus had the reputation of being a devil at the wheel. The heavier the wind, the more he piled on the canvas. He wasn't reckless, but he knew his business well enough to make decisions that would not be obvious to lesser sailors. As fishing captains went he was a small man. Most skippers were large men who did not hesitate to enforce an order with a fist if the need arose, especially when

18

Lunenburg for Vessel

He was a real Schoonerman + understood the Bluenose + could make her go

the survival of their vessel or their men was at stake. But Walters had his own weaponry and was know as much for his stinging tongue as for his love of full sail. Men twice his size were known to wince and go below rather than stand up to one of his tongue-lashings.

The races, of course, were the talk of the town. For many years there had been a fishermen's festival in the fall of the year, a sort of carnival to celebrate the survival of those who had risked life and limb all summer on the Banks. Dory races, swimming meets, ox-driving contests, all sorts of games of skill and endurance were played. People came into Lunenburg from surrounding farms on foot, by horse, and by oxcart. Families got together; friends from far away made it the occasion for the yearly visit; there were parties, marching bands, parades, and sermons. Everyone was glad of the chance to rise above the routine worries of a fisherman's life, but the fact that this year the races were to be an international event, with a big cash prize and unheard-of publicity, turned the fishermen's fall festival into an opportunity for ordinary folks to see themselves and their style of life as something unique and wonderful in the eyes of the world.

The first elimination races were held just outside Halifax harbor on October 11, 1920. In spite of the morning chill, the wharves and breakwaters were lined with spectators. Young men climbed to the crosstrees of anchored ships; others took up posts on the roofs of harborside warehouses; still others brought telescopes and racecourse maps to lookout points farther south along the shore. Everyone who had a boat to watch from brought it as close to the finish line as he could.

Angus had entered the *Gilbert B. Walters,* and there were a great many Lunenburgers who banked on his winning. He was running slightly behind the *Delawana* when, on the last leg of the race, his topmast broke. *Delawana* beat him by five minutes, and Capt. Tommy Himmelman won the honor of representing Canada in the forthcoming contest for the trophy. But Angus was the unofficial hero of the town.

Every shift of wind, every small maneuver, every decision and alternative was duly noted and debated by a populace in which even the little boys had suddenly become sailing experts.

The talk was great sport—almost as much as the race itself—but the fun lasted only a single day. Word came on October 12 that Capt. Calvin Lohnes, whose vessel had finished seventh in the elimination races, had sailed his last race. On his way home to LaHave, a town just south of Lunenburg, he was struck by the main boom of his vessel, knocked overboard, and drowned.

Was it a warning, some wondered, that the sea was not to be mocked by mere men? Perhaps it was, for Captain Lohnes's death was only the first of a frightening number of men and ships who reached for the fishermen's trophy and lost it to the cruel sea.

Yet, if fishing had come to a standstill on every occasion of violent death, there would have been no fish caught, and no man would ever have put to sea. Violent death was a condition of the fisherman's life—and life, under any circumstances, had to continue.

A week later, the American entry, *Esperanto,* breezed into Halifax harbor. Like most of the American entries in the schooner races, she was considerably smaller than the Canadian *Delawana,* but she had a great skipper at her wheel. He was Capt. Marty Welch, a "whitewashed Yankee," Nova Scotian by birth and American by adoption. Like his old friend and frequent rival Angus Walters, Marty also had a reputation as a great sail carrier. Until he brought *Esperanto* up to Halifax, he had never skippered this particular vessel. Though *Esperanto* was a new experience for him, he never surrendered her wheel during the entire series.

Esperanto was an old veteran. She had served fourteen hard years on the Banks when her chance came to represent her fleet. She arrived, fresh from the Banks, still wearing her limp, stretched-out sails, but her send-off from Gloucester had been nothing short of spectacular. Thousands of people had lined the wharves to wave and wish her good luck, and the most able skippers in Gloucester served as her crew. She beat *Delawana* in the first race by eighteen minutes.

Delawana was no clipper either, and she was loaded down with far too much stone ballast. Tommy Himmelman's crew removed as much ballast as they dared, and in the second race,

Born + raised in, Digby nova Scotia a great sail Carrier fisherman

20

Delawana lead her American rival right up to the last. But, in a daring dash across *Delawana's* weather, the American crossed the finish line seven minutes ahead of the Canadian.

She skedaddled home to Gloucester with 4000 hard-earned Canadian cash dollars, and the four-foot loving cup, to the greatest reception ever bestowed upon a fishing vessel in the history of her town. There were gold watches for the crew, banquets, receptions, a giant show with an all-star cast. Even Calvin Coolidge, that most close-lipped of American Presidents, opened his mouth long enough to say, "The victory was a triumph for Americanism."

Though neither of these vessels was spectacularly fast, this first race probably came closer to the original purpose and intention of the founding committees than any race that was to follow. Both vessels were in working gear, both were seasoned saltbankers, neither had been built with an eye to the races, and they were, by any measure, hardworking representatives of the industry, both north of the border and south.

Gay as the spirit was down in Gloucester, however, up in Nova Scotia there was much grinding of teeth. Revenge was the order of the day.

Tommy Himmelman
was one of Four Brothers
all Fisherman from N. S.

Chapter Four

Senator Dennis called his friends together again. The cup had to come home to Nova Scotia. They would build a vessel to beat the best that the Americans could put together, and they wouldn't spare in the doing of it, either. She would stand for all that was glorious in the shipbuilding province of Nova Scotia. This vessel was going to be named *Bluenose.*

Although the then current price of cod hardly justified a big investment in a saltbanker, the decision was made and the money pledged. Fully rigged, *Bluenose* ended up costing $35,000, or nearly twice the cost of an average saltbanker, but she was Canadian royalty, and the best was not too good for her.

The Halifax men went down to Lunenburg and asked Angus Walters if he would join them as skipper. "Not unless I have the controlling share in her," he said. For Angus was well pleased with the *Gilbert B. Walters.* She was a big, sturdy ship, and she had paid her cost three times over in the short time he had owned her. He knew as well as any man in Lunenburg that no two vessels came off the stocks exactly alike and that the difference between any two of them could be as drastic as it was unpredictable. He might be trading a fine, dependable boat for a temperamental prima donna.

The usual practice in financing sailing ships was to divide their ownership into sixty-four shares, or "pieces." Usually the largest shareholder got his name on the prow, which is how some of the Lunenburg vessels came to have names like *Eva V. Culp,*

Sadie E. Knickle, Annie L. Spindler (or the one on the septuagenarian Gloucester schooner *Effie M. Morrisey,* still going strong at seventy-four years of age). But because *Bluenose* was going to cost much more than an ordinary vessel, a corporation was formed and shares were sold at $100 apiece. Walters held the largest number of shares, enough to give him the final word in her building and management.

The committee commissioned a yacht designer named William Roue to submit a plan for *Bluenose.* Roue had designed *Zetes,* a racing sloop which won three cups in her heyday in 1910. Roue's first submission was turned down by the committee because the proposed vessel was too big. Instead of cutting down on all the specifications, he adapted the *Zetes* design for *Bluenose.* The queen would inherit her fastest features from *Zetes.*

Seen from the side, she seemed to be "all bow and no midships." She was so smoothly tapered toward the stern that her hull never left any dead water. (Dead water is water which eddies around the stern and tends to drag the vessel backward, especially when it is making little headway.)

She had a very short keel for a vessel her size, only fifty feet of a total length of one hundred forty-three, so that two thirds of her hull was overhang. Roue kept her inside ballast—and consequently her center of gravity—as low as possible by adding reinforced concrete to the top of her keel. She had the typical spoon bow of the fisherman's profile, originally introduced by the Boston yacht designer, B. B. Crowninshield. This profile lengthened her at the waterline. It is a surprising principle of hydrodynamics that the longer a vessel is at the water line, the greater her speed.

A last-minute change added eighteen inches to her bow freeboard, which is the part of the deck farthest forward. The purpose of this change was actually to give her crew in the fo'c'sle more headroom. It kept her men drier on deck than they were topside on most saltbankers, and while it did not add to her speed, it gave her bow a pert, uptilted look that distinguished her from all other vessels of her type.

Aside from these particular features, *Bluenose* was a standard fishing vessel, inside and out. Her deck plan was the same

23

as any schooner's: anchors and cables at the prow, windlass, fore-mast, a nest of four dories on either side of her midships, main-mast, fish-cleaning equipment, "gurry kid," cabin, wheel and wheelbox.

Belowdecks, her forward section was the crew's quarters, known in nautical language as the "forecastle," or "fo'c'sle." Despite the name, the crew's accommodations were not palatial, but were highly ingenious: sleeping bunks lining the hull, with small lockers for the fisherman's belongings; then the galley, or ship's kitchen and pantry, with its stove bolted to the deck, and movable iron rods to keep the pots from jumping about. A big table between the bunks served for all meals. Unlike the procedure followed on other fishing vessels, the Banks skipper, his mate, and the most experienced men aboard generally ate in the forward section at the same table as the men, although at an earlier sitting than the rest of the crew. On tern schooners and other vessels the cook carried the captain's food across the deck to the after cabin in what was called a "dog basket," and the captain and mate dined together in the splendid solitude of their own quarters.

Separating the fo'c'sle from the captain's cabin at the after end of the vessel was the hold, actually the business section of the boat. Here were the great pens in which salt and fish were stored. They opened to the deck by means of hatches—rectangular holes—each with a cover.

Farthest aft was the cabin, which provided the captain with slightly more sleeping room than the crew members and also contained a small desk for charts, instruments, compass, log, and so on.

The bottom layer of the vessel's hull held the ballast—either pig iron or stones—and beneath it, of course, lay the keel.

Her sail plan, too, was standard for a saltbanker: Jib, jumbo, foresail, and mainsail were her "lowers." Four smaller sails flew from her topmasts when she was in full rig, but the most characteristic was the triangular fisherman's staysail, used to give the vessel stability while she was anchored on the Banks.

The construction of a wooden vessel is a fascinating process. Roughly speaking, it is built, like any other structure, from

24

Iron
+
Cement

I think she means storm trysail
The Fisherman staysail is four sided

the bottom to the top. First the keel is laid, then the ribs of the vessel are put in place. The outer shell, or hull, comes next, and then the planking of the deck. The saltbankers had to be strong enough to withstand a broadside attack by a comber, one of those five-mile-long waves that build up across a thousand miles or so of open ocean. When the fragile human life within the hull of a vessel struck broadside by such a sea could be the carpenter's own son or nephew, as was the case with so many of the Lunenburg shipwrights, that carpenter took all the time and care he needed to do the job as well as possible.

A vessel is launched quite some time before it is completed. Generally the painted hull is towed to another wharf, one equipped with block and tackle for installing spars and rigging. The most crucial of these operations is the "stepping of the mast."

The masts of a sailing vessel are not fastened permanently to the vessel by screws or bolts, both because they often need replacement and because their separateness provides greater flexibility. Instead the masts are inserted between two huge sets of blocks. The lower set is attached to the keel; the upper is attached to the deck. The mast is held upright by wire cables called "stays." One set, called "forestays," run from the top of the mast to the forward and after ends of the vessel. Another set, called "shrouds," brace the mast by running down to either side of the vessel's hull. When a mast snapped—and it frequently did —it was possible to release its terrible drag or pull on the vessel by simply cutting the stays and the shrouds and letting the mast fall. But "cutting out the spars" was a last-ditch measure which left a vessel helpless, and no captain resorted to such a thing except in a very last extremity.

Bluenose was a big vessel, even for a saltbanker. From bow to stern she measured 143 feet, with another seventeen feet added for her bowsprit. Altogether she was nearly as long as an average city block. Fitted with her topmasts, she reached one hundred twenty-six feet from deck to pennant, or about the height of a twelve-story building. She was built at the yards of Smith & Rhuland, a company with long experience with two-masted fishing schooners. *Bluenose* was their hundred and twentieth vessel.

This argument with the foreman was about her spars.

While she was under construction early in 1921, Angus Walters was the informal overseer. He was in fact a terror to the shipwrights, poking into every operation, arguing for quality and expressing an opinion about everything that went into the building of the ship. He was not an easy man to work for. Once a dispute with a foreman made him so angry that he stalked out, vowing never to set foot in the yard again, and Smith & Rhuland could do what they bloody well pleased with the half-finished hull. He was through, and that was the end of it! A week later he was back—on his own terms, of course—and the work proceeded.

Long after *Bluenose* had become a legend, people around Lunenburg looked for exotic explanations of her uncanny sailing qualities. They spoke of her having been built out in the open, rather than in a shed, remembering that a particularly hard frost had hit that spring, a frost which they claimed had "set her timbers." Both her designer and her skipper were outraged by such talk. Roue maintained of course that she was fast because he had designed her to be fast. Angus believed that the crucial element in her construction was that her masts had been "stepped mathematically perfect." True, the stepping of the masts is one of the most delicate operations of shipbuilding, for enormous weights and tensions must be adjusted to a hair. Probably the mathematical perfection to which Walters referred could not have been calculated by any mechanical means. Without her topmasts, *Bluenose,* like her fellow fishermen, was a bit squat in appearance. But with her topmasts, she simply *looked* perfect, and she very nearly was.

The launching of *Bluenose* on March 26, 1921, was quite a contrast to the ceremony that had attended the laying of her keel some months earlier. Canada's governor-general, the Duke of Devonshire, had been invited to attend the first party and to drive home the ceremonial spike which symbolized the start of construction. Apparently the duke had begun to fortify himself for the effort some hours before the party began, for he had great difficulty connecting the mallet with the spike. Steadier hands than his finally drove the spike home, and Lunenburg was glad to discover that the king's own representative was a "reg'l'r fella."

26

There was plenty of Nelsons Blood Rum on hand at keying & launching.

If the keel-laying ceremony had been an occasion for embarrassed hilarity, the launching itself was not. A launching is a little like a wedding: It represents the end of the beginning and, in a certain sense, the beginning of the end. It is a time when people look back and a time when they look ahead as well. Mostly, however, people think about life itself at weddings and ship launchings, and even the strongest men can grow misty-eyed.

No one could know the character of the great dark form which lay imprisoned and obscured by the scaffolding. Poised at the edge of the sea, her homely beauty might have moved even an indifferent spectator, if there had been one. But everyone wanted to see how she met the water. Some vessels when they slipped free, nosed toward the land as if they were reluctant to go to sea. One of *Bluenose*'s later competitors was so badly damaged at her launching that months of repairs were needed to set her innards to rights. Occasionally a vessel has been known to roll over on its beam-ends when it is released from restraint. For once the struts are removed, and before the towlines take control, the hull is entirely on its own, with only the force of gravity to draw it into its natural element.

There were many government officials present on that blustery day in March; visiting dignitaries from as far west as Toronto had come to see the launching. They moved among the Lunenburgers in the muddy shipyard, stepping over lumber, trying to avoid puddles, pulling their scarves closer and their hats down over their ears, talking, comparing, speculating, remembering. Lunenburgers cast a skeptical eye on the visitors, shrugged at all the fuss, which wasn't much by any standards, and shared the laconic satisfaction with which the clerk in Smith & Rhuland's modest office noted in Palmer script this entry in his ledger: "Vessel Number 120 launched this day. Name: *Bluenose.*" Number 119 had gone before. Number 121 would come after. It was the everyday business of the town, and there was no call to get foolish about it.

There were a few short speeches, the familiar tinkling of glass as the bottle was broken against her bow, and then the familiar cries, "Wedge up!" and "Knock down dogs!" A dozen sledgehammers struck away her fetters. For a long moment *Blue-*

nose hesitated. Then, with gathering momentum, she slid down the ways and entered the tide with a deep, grand curtsy—a bride meeting her bridegroom.

The crowd applauded and then fell silent, for she was beginning to move again of her own accord. Turning, turning, her bow scanned the harbor's rim, saluting first the shipyards; then the monument at Rouses' Brook where the first of the German settlers had come ashore; then the old sailors' home at the top of the hill, paying tribute in turn to the unassuming integrity of the men who had made her and to the great past which lay behind her. Then she paused, her bow steadfast at last, like the needle of a compass pointing true north. She paused and nodded toward the open sea beyond the harbor, saying yes to her destiny.

The waiting crowd, diffuse before, moved as one to the water's edge and broke into cheers. "She's sniffin' the sea breeze! She'll be a lucky ship!"

⚓

Three weeks later her masts were stepped, her rigging was lashed into place, and ten thousand square feet of sail was bent upon her spars.

Angus Walters took her out for her first run. "I thought she had a darned good move to her," he commented cautiously.

According to the rules of the competition a vessel had to put in at least one full season of fishing on the Banks in order to qualify for the races. After all, the serious purpose of the competition was to improve the design and efficiency of fishing schooners. With the steep investment in her construction, *Bluenose* would have to catch plenty of fish to pay back her owners.

Angus did not waste any time in signing on a crew and getting away to the Banks. He took down her topmasts, stowed her racing sails, and set out to catch cod.

On his way out to the Banks, he sighted the *Gilbert B. Walters* and called to her new captain to give him a "hook." The captain agreed, and both crews leaped to the game. The *Gilbert B. Walters* was no match for the blue-black beauty, whose sturdy sides had yet to be scarred by dories dropping into the sea. *Bluenose* darted ahead like a gust of wind, leaving the *Gilbert B. Walters* to trail in her wake.

28

Hoisting the main throat Hallyard
4 men also on other side of
mast on Peak hallyard

Chapter Five

Cod fishing had never been so good as it was the first few years after World War I, when Lunenburg skippers Knickle, Himmelman, Mosher, Cook, Spindler, and Walters were breaking records. When Angus's father, Capt. Elias Walters, had taken Angus, then thirteen years old, on his first trip to the Banks in 1895, he'd broken the town's record with a hundred-ton catch. A quarter of a century later, in 1919, the son staggered the town with a catch four times that size.

Larger vessels and bigger carrying capacity were only one part of the story. When *Bluenose* began her career, there were many more fish swimming around Nova Scotia and Newfoundland than there had been for a long time. Four years of war had given the fish a chance to graze and reproduce on those underwater plateaus, undisturbed but for the occasional torpedoed fishing vessel that sank slowly into their midst. The war which wiped out so many fishermen had, by the same token, greatly multiplied the population of fish. Even with the loss of a third of her vessels, Lunenburg was landing bonanza catches.

Methods of catching fish were changing too. When Sebastian Cabot first fished on the Banks, back in 1497, the cod were so thick a man could scarcely row a boat through their schools. Cabot's men caught cod by tossing a basket, weighted with a stone, into the sea. Later, fishermen dropped baited lines over the vessel's side—a method called handlining. Essentially handlining is what any boy does when he is confronted by a pond in which fish are said to swim; it was the only method used in Lunenburg until quite late in the 1800s.

But around 1850, a good number of New England fishermen began to fish by another method. It was much more dangerous, but it multiplied the catch many times over. It was called dory fishing.

A dory is a small boat about twice the size of a rowboat, but narrower on the bottom and higher on the sides. Schooners sailed out to the Banks carrying six to twelve dories nested on their decks. When they reached the fishing grounds, often two or three weeks after clearing port, depending on the weather and the availability of bait, each of the vessels anchored, the fisherman's staysail was set, and the dories were lowered over the vessel's side. The fishermen jumped into them, took the trawl lines and bait buckets handed them by the skipper or the cook, and rowed off to catch cod.

Some times they carried 18 dories

rn or dying sl not herman tayol

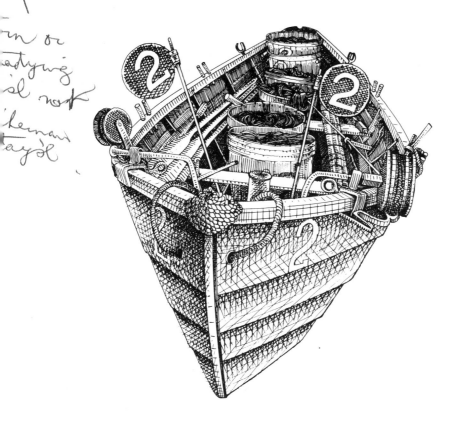

Lunenburgers did not go in for dory fishing until more than thirty years after the New Englanders began, probably for the simple reason that no Lunenburger had ever done it before. Lunenburg was a tradition-bound town. Then, in 1872, a Lunenburg captain named Ben Anderson decided to have a go at the Yankee method. Anderson's chief delight in life, next to catching fish, lay in shocking the conservatives. He was known to have taken on supplies on the eastern side of a wharf rather than on the western, to have loaded up on a Friday, even to have taken on supplies on the thirteenth day of a month. People said of Ben, "There's no tellin' what sort of foolishness that man'll be into next. Probably catch fish in dories!" And, of course, his scandalized neighbors were perfectly right. Ben Anderson took four dories and thirteen fishermen out to Grand Bank on his vessel *Dielytris,* and his catch made Lunenburg's eyes pop.

His 92-year old niece, Mape Anderson, who still lives in Lunenburg, says, "They all used to go out together, just so far, and then come back. Then one time when the others stopped, Ben just kept on going." He'd probably had a poor catch close to home and did not want to come back empty-hulled. Never before had Lunenburgers fished the farthest bank, but once a Lunenburger set the precedent, all the Lunenburg vessels began to carry dories and fish far from port. Pretty soon they were the best in the business.

Early dory fishing was also by handline. The fishermen dropped six or seven lines over the side of the dory instead of off the side of the vessel, and they made good catches, too, for cod seemed to be attracted by the movement of a "squid-jigger," a funny-looking metal hook with small spikes at the end of it.

By the time *Bluenose* was built, however, nearly all the Lunenburgers had switched to the long-line trawl. Instead of dropping baited hooks one at a time over the dory's side, the long-line trawl put almost sixteen hundred baited hooks down on the floor of the Banks in one operation. A trawl is just a piece of rope a mile and a half long to which small, short ropes called ganges (pronounced gén-jiz) are tied at intervals of every five feet. At the end of each gange is a baited hook. The heavy trawl line is attached at either end to a hollow keg, with a numbered flag, to mark its place in the water.

The dorymen, two to a boat, sometimes worked as far as five miles away from their vessel. Most of them carried a single sail, and if the wind was right they would sail down the trawl, paying out the line as they went. At other times they would row. The place of honor was held by the forward doryman, who stood at the prow, lifted the coiled trawl line from its bucket with a heaving stick and payed it out into the sea. Laying trawl required great care and skill, for a stiff breeze or a bouncing dory could plunge a hook into the doryman's hand or eye as easily as into the water.

When the trawl lay on the ocean floor, the dorymen either rested on their oars for a smoke or returned to their vessel for a "mug-up." About an hour later they would "underrun the trawl," hauling up one end, putting the dory under it, gaffing the ~~or slatting~~ fish off the hook, and rebaiting as they worked their way down the trawl. While the forward doryman gaffed, the second man

33

Pie
or
Doughnuts & Coffee or Tea
The Cooks made their own bread, Pies & Doughnuts

rebaited and dropped the line back into the water. If one fish dangled on every fifteenth hook, the dory might bring in a ton or even two tons of fish from a single set, but that took extraordinary luck. If the fish were biting, the dories would rebait and leave the trawls where they were. If they were not, the skipper ran up his flag, the dorymen picked up their lines and returned to the schooner, or—if they had made a "flying set"—the vessel itself "broke out the hook," or weighed anchor, and scudded down the wind to pick up the dories to take them elsewhere. (In a flying set the vessel towed the dories behind it, dropped them off one at a time, and picked them up when the trawl lines had been retrieved.)

Generally the dories made four sets a day. With such an expenditure of time, effort, and bait, a skipper had to be pretty sure he was "putting his men on fish" before he gave the order to lower dories. Like any experienced fisherman, Angus could tell from studying the stuff clinging to the tallow end of the heaving lead what sort of fish the trawls would bring up, even before the first dory went banging over the side. If the bottom was sandy, there might be cod. If the tallow came up clean, they were over rock, and there would be none. When the cod had been running well and dogfish turned up, the wise fisherman wasted no time picking up the dories and moving, for dogfish always chased away the cod.

The cod is a greedy, stupid fish which will bite on anything, even on an unbaited hook. It is a ground feeder and has no tolerance for a swift journey to the water's surface. It comes up limp, stunned, and airblown, like a man with the bends. Halibut on the other hand never takes a hook without a fight. Dorymen carried a club called a halibut stick, used to wallop a halibut on the head before hauling it into the dory. A hundred-pound halibut could do a lot of damage thrashing around in a small boat full of wet fish. Usually the second doryman lashed it by the tail to a thwart lest the knockout might prove impermanent.

Of course, trawl lines picked up hake, pollack, and haddock as well as cod. Everything that was neither cod nor halibut was called "shack," and brought a lower price. Not all the fish were marketable, and some were a downright menace, like sharks which broke the trawls and sometimes snapped off a fisherman's hand as well. Sometimes the trawls were snarled by passing whales. Often steam vessels cut the trawl lines, and on occasion other schooners ruined a set, which was why skippers looked for solitary berths whenever they could be found. Then too, currents shifted the lines or caused them to drift, or anchors came loose. With twenty miles of trawl laid out on the ocean floor each time his men made a set, a skipper had to know just what he was about.

When the weather was calm and the fishing good, the dories even fished in the darkness, with only a small kerosene flare on the dory's gunwales (gunnels) to light their work.

SPLITTING

But listen to an old-timer tell about dory fishing, as related by James H. Marsh in his *Fishermen of Lunenburg* (Holt, Rinehart and Winston of Canada, Ltd., 1968):

> "You'd go out in the mornin', waves tall as ships, in a small dory 'bout as big as a rowboat. For hours you'd bob around on the waves, never seein' the main wessel. Wintertime it were severe cold every day. Your face were thick with ice. Your hands froze to your gloves. The winds were always strong. The seas were always high. I lost relatives and friends. You never knew if you were comin' back."

Like most youngsters in Lunenburg, Angus Walters had shoveled salt at the dockside for a summer before his father allowed him to come aboard on his first trip. His job, then, was as a "throater" in the dressing crew. For the saltbankers not only caught the fish, but because it was so perishable, they performed the first step in processing as well. As soon as the last dory had been picked up, kerosene lamps were lighted, trestle tables set up, and the job of "dressing down the catch" was begun. Fish heads were lopped off, bellies split, the liver was carefully removed (remember cod-liver oil?) and the rest of the fish's innards were ripped out. After a fast rinse in seawater, the flattened fish slid down a chute into the hold, where it was carefully laid to rest, head to tail, between heavy layers of salt. If the vessel was approaching a port, all the waste was stored on deck in a square wooden box called the "gurry kid." This was also the place where the trawl buckets and dory gear were stored when the dories were not in use. Otherwise waste was simply shoveled overboard.

The throater was the man who slit the fish open with a very sharp knife, and as the youngest aboard, Angus probably had the job of chasing off the petrels as well. These were seabirds which dived down on the deck to snatch the offal. No fisherman would think of harming a petrel, for they were emissaries of hope and good luck. But they could make dressing down quite an adventure.

A throater came across some pretty strange things when he opened up cod: oilcans, boots, scissors, keys—once someone even found a book inside a cod's belly! Dressing down could take the last strength out of a man as well. Exhausted by a long day in a

37

dory, his hands bloated or infected with sea boils, working with razor-sharp instruments on a heaving deck, the fisherman who escaped injury was rare. Sometimes there were freak accidents, as when a salter, working in the hold by the light of a single candle stuck into the timbers, was buried alive under tons of fish when the vessel lurched.

On young Angus's very first trip, the cook on his father's vessel was washed overboard. Captain Elias put a dory over the side at once, but it was dark and stormy, and he hadn't much hope. The flares on deck scarcely touched the blackness of the water. Suddenly one of the dorymen spotted a derby bobbing on the water. "Poor Cook!" he cried, and rowed as fast as he could to pick up this pitiful memento of a departed friend. Lifting the derby from the water, he discovered that the cook was still under it. He pulled him out and revived him aboard the schooner. The cook lived to sail and cook under that derby for many years thereafter.

To the unpracticed eye, the fishing grounds were like any other expanse of ocean, though a sharp observer might notice a slight difference in the movement of water over the Banks, or take note of the dense clouds of seabirds hovering over their food supply. But the saltbank skippers were in a class by themselves when it came to navigation. Long after the navy and the merchant marine had started counting on the sextant and the chronometer to determine their location, the saltbankers still "navigated by the lead." They determined where they were by measuring depth of water. The Banks lay thirty-five to forty fathoms beneath the surface of the sea. Reefs might be at depths as shallow as ten fathoms. Then there were deep pits in the ocean bottom, with names like the Whale Hole, the Gully, the Barrel, or the Hogshead. Today the Banks have been as well surveyed and charted as the land areas around them. But in the 1920s few skippers even kept a log, and they made do with the roughest charts, going on the experience of their own lifetime and the talk of other men. "I don't need no 'nourse'!" was the proud boast of many a skipper, referring to a navigator skilled in the use of the sextant.

38

When Angus was fifteen, his father judged him a promising enough lad to be allowed to go out as junior man in a dory. But Angus's greatest reward was always a chance to steer the vessel. He volunteered for the dogwatches, never missing a chance to take another man's turn to control the great white bird, no matter how early or late the opportunity arrived. By the time he had become master of *Bluenose,* there was not very much he did not know about the handling of a schooner in any kind of weather.

While his vessel was at sea, the skipper kept to himself, talking very little, guarding his knowledge and even his hunches with jealous secrecy, for when a man became a highliner, all the boats in the fleet would follow his lead. It was a canny fellow who knew how to give his hangers-on the slip. The secrecy with which skippers conducted themselves had a very long history. Even on the first known map, drawn by the Portuguese mapmaker Cortino in 1504, the Banks are roughly sketched shallows called "Codfishland." Maps like this were preserved only because they were kept under lock and key, available only to the monarchs who commissioned them, men like Henry the Navigator of Portugal. Such markings were like those on pirates' maps, with "X" marking the treasure. At that, the general location of "Codfishland" was probably known to the more daring fishermen for more than a hundred years before it turned up on Cortino's map.

In the days before radio, even baiting up called for frequent dodging and dissembling. Cod was caught with herring for bait, and sometimes a skipper had to visit several ports before he found it. Herring, capelin, and squid were all good bait and had to be purchased, fresh, from the Magdalen Islands or from some of the Newfoundland outports. Once he'd baited up, a skipper was not likely to tell his competition where the herring was running or what price he'd paid for it. But the practiced banksmen could nearly tell by a glance what lay in another skipper's hold, where he was headed and why, and what he would probably find when he got there.

A thousand considerations were always joggling about in a skipper's head: his estimate of the weather, the size of the catch in his hold, the number of days he had been out, the price he was likely to fetch at the dock, the condition of his vessel and his men. He read the set of the tides, the lay of the wind, the character of clouds and the behavior of birds as if they were a chart, assigning to each observation the weight of his years of experience. The number of times he made the right decision to go or stay, to try another berth or run home with what he had, to gamble on danger for the sake of a good fare—all these judgments rested entirely with the captain.

In Lunenburg it was the practice for all the vessels to receive the same price for their catches. But in other ports, a skipper might have to scratch to sell his catch, sometimes hitting the market late, after the price had dropped. Speed in bringing in the catch could make the difference between a profit and a loss, and this was the basic reason for building fast schooners in the first place.

To the doryman setting his trawl by the light of a small flare, or rowing through a blinding snowstorm toward the place where he believed his vessel to be, the schooner was a haven and a refuge. But the vessel itself was not really "in" any place at all. "Place" is a word which describes something on land. At sea there is no such thing as place; there is only direction. And whether the vessel was in fact a haven was an altogether relative matter. It was far better to be aboard a vessel than in an open dory, to be sure, but hardly what a landsman would think of as "safe."

The fishermen took enormous pride in their ability to withstand danger and discomfort and to take them in stride. On the saltbanker *Mary L. McKay,* a boarding sea crashed through a half-opened hatch, putting out the fire in the galley stove and flooding the fo'c'sle. The ship keeled over on her beam-ends, pitching sleeping men from their bunks, hurling pots, pans, pitchers, plates, and potatoes across the galley. The bos'n fought to get down the companionway, both his trouser legs ripped off by the wind. The cook gripped the railing above his stove as boxes, tools, mittens, and pillows surged against his knees. Peering through the clouds of steam from his hissing stove, he inquired, "Hey, Charlie, how's the weather?"

Next to the skipper, the cook was the most important man aboard a saltbanker, perhaps not in his rating or his pay but in what he added to the quality of life aboard ship. The men on a saltbanker ate often and they ate well, and most cooks kept their galleys clean and their stoves going at all hours of the day and night.

The working day aboard a Banks schooner began at 3:30 or 4:00 in the morning with a quick "mug-up"—a drink of hot tea or coffee—and a scramble to get the dories into the water an hour before dawn. Because the weather changed so often, it was important to use as much daylight as possible. If a dory got lost in snow or fog it was safer to be on the lookout with several hours of daylight ahead than at nightfall.

Fog was an ever-present danger on the Banks and accounted for more deaths than any other sort of weather. Still, sinister, and blinding, it shut down like a curtain, cutting the doryman off from the only means short of intuition of finding his way back to his vessel. This fog resulted from the meeting of the warm air of the northward-flowing Gulf Stream with the icy waters of the southward-flowing Laborador current. These two great parallel currents flowing in opposite directions created the Banks in millennia past and moved so close to one another, in such distinct patterns, that a vessel could have its prow in one and its stern in the other.

Old-time dorymen used to boast that they could smell their way back to the vessel "t'ru any t'ick o' fog." But equipped as they were with only a small jug of water, a thimbleful of rum, and maybe a conch shell or a small megaphone, there were many stray dorymen who simply died of thirst, starvation or exposure. Fog also concealed vessels from one another, shrouding the movements of the deadly schedule-driven steamships whose route to Europe cut directly across the Banks like a butcher's cleaver. Under their impact, a fishing schooner splintered like a matchstick. Whole crews were abandoned without recognition or succor from merchantmen and mail packets hell-bent on "making time." Slower-moving than steamers but nearly as treacherous

In the latter years of dory traveling the dories
Carried little radios so the schooners
could get a Bearing Signal on them if need
to

were the icebergs and growlers that drifted south on the Labrador current to terrorize dorymen.

In the last years of dory fishing, some of the vessels began to
carry small cannons, firing them to help the dorymen find their
way back by sound. But the number of times dories missed their
vessels by a few yards to be lost forever will never be known.

Fog, of course, was not the only danger. With more than a
ton of wet fish sliding around in an open boat on a rough sea,
many men simply lost their footing and slipped into the sea.
When a man fell overboard, sometimes the air trapped in his
oilskins was the only thing that kept him afloat until someone
picked him up, since traditionally fishermen never learned to
swim (maybe because Nova Scotian waters are cold, even in summer, and maybe because when the weather was fine, fishermen
were too busy fishing). If his dory capsized he might have been
able to seize the plug strap at its bottom and hang on. A few men
saved themselves in this way, but there are more stories like this
one told by a Lunenburger. Reaching through the darkness of
memory, he says, "There was the two of us standin' in the dory,
laughin' and talkin', and then Fred slips on a net and all of a
sudden he's gone. Just gone." That particular Fred left a widow
and five orphans behind when he sank to the bottom of the sea.

Each trip to the Banks taught its own lesson in survival, for
circumstances were never exactly the same twice. When a man
signed on to a schooner for a "hitch" or a "sight," he knew that
his chances of returning alive depended upon the soundness of
the skipper's judgments, the seaworthiness of the vessel, the
whims of wind and weather, and just plain luck. Whether or not
he made any money from his work was another story. The contract on a fishing vessel was more generous to the men, in some
respects, than it was on other types of seagoing ships. Lunenburgers always fished "on shares," rather than "by count," which
meant that each crew member received the same pay as all the
other crew members—a share in the sale price of the catch—but
the reckoning was not made until the owner's expenses for food,
bait, and maintenance, and his profit and the skipper's share (usually a third) were deducted. Each trip was reported like this:
"The schooner ——— landed a fare of 13,000 lbs. halibut, 45,-

ooo shack (mixed fish), 20,000 salt cod. The ten day trip stocked $3720, and the share was $76.00 per man." That particular trip was noticeably profitable, enough to get itself reported in the newspapers.

Not all the disasters and near disasters on the Banks were the result of natural forces. Sometimes it was man's own miscalculations, the straying of a skipper's attention, or some unaccountable quirk in the mind of a helmsman that brought a host of men to grief.

Such a time as that nearly spelled the end of *Bluenose* on a clear night on her very first trip to the Banks. Captain Walters told of it in his own words excerpted from G. J. Gillespie's *Bluenose Skipper* (Brunswick Press, 1955):

> "On our maiden voyage of the *Bluenose* after taking bait on board we anchored. After our first fishing, one fine night, the watch came down and called me about 2:00 A.M. He said there was another vessel approaching us. When I came and looked at her—I had my binoculars with me—I saw that it was not a fishing vessel coming to speak to us but a full-rigged ship. I kept watching her and it appeared to me there was no watch on this ship at the time, as she appeared she was going to almost cut us down. She got so close that I said to the watch, 'Blow the foghorn!' Still there appeared to be no attraction. She got so close that I told the watch to call the crew out and get the dories overboard because it was beginning to look very serious. When the dories was over, I jumped in one with two of the crew, and I rowed over alongside the ship which wasn't very far away from us and I thought I could climb aboard of her. But I found I could not get up because she was very high out of the water. I sung out and somebody on deck answered me. I asked him what he intended to do, 'run us down?' Could he not see our riding lights and the vessel right there?
>
> "He said that his ship could not keep off. I said, 'If she will not keep off why do you not back your yards and let her drift away from us?'
>
> "One thing I noticed when I rowed around the bow of the *Bluenose,* I noticed the tide was going astern. That was a help to us. After that we rowed alongside the *Bluenose* but, of course, we weren't going aboard because I was certain she was going to be run down. What actually put her clear of us, that she did not cut us in two, is more than I can say. That full-rigged ship just cleared us by inches."

43

Lunenburg fishermen took most of their catch due east of Nova Scotia, on Sable Island Bank, Middle, Western, Banquereau and sometimes the Grand Bank. Dangerous as their work might have been on the open sea, most vessels met their end quite close to shore, racking up on the jagged rocks of the underwater reefs which jutted out, lethal and invisible, to ensnare them. Even worse than rocky reefs were the constantly shifting sands of Sable Island, "the graveyard of the Atlantic." More than three hundred vessels were know to have been lost there in a single century, and how many others broke up on her torture rack will forever be a question because too often there were no survivors. Caught upon those toils and foundering, a vessel might roll back and forth over miles of sand until the men within her were literally skinned alive.

As if one such tragedy were not enough, it sometimes happened that a wrecked vessel became not only its own sepulcher but the instrument of another vessel's death as well. A skipper might know the shape of the reefs well enough, but he could never predict when the ocean currents might sweep the hull of a drowned ship to the sea's surface to smash against his own ship.

Bluenose had just landed her first fare when word came to Lunenburg, by way of Halifax, that *Esperanto,* pride of the Gloucester fleet and winner of the first international fishermen's trophy, had collided with the submerged wreck of another American vessel, the *S.S. State of Virginia,* off Sable Island. *Esperanto* went down in ten fathoms of water, with 140,000 pounds of fish in her hold. Her crew of twenty-one scrambled into the dories and were picked up three hours later by Capt. Alden Geele, at the helm of the Gloucester schooner *Elsie.* He landed the men at Halifax.

Later, three attempts were made to raise *Esperanto.* The first two were nearly successful, for her topmasts still showed above the water. The third attempt was beset by storms, fogs, and raging tides. Before the Gloucestermen could go back for a fourth try, word came that *Esperanto* had broken up and her wreckage was drifting ashore.

Chapter Six

At the end of September, 1921, *Bluenose* picked up her skirts and hurried home. She was not the only vessel to quit the Banks early that season. Usually the fishermen worked until the end of October, when the weather bore down with such earnestness that only desperate men dared to defy it. But that fall, instead of making their fourth trip, eight vessels headed home early to spruce up for the races. Six were from Lunenburg, one from Shelburne, and one from LaHave.

Bluenose had landed a large enough catch that summer to keep her skipper's reputation as a highliner untarnished. Now Angus took his new boat into the shipyard for a thorough inspection of her bottom, for barnacles and seaweed clinging to the hull would slow her down. Her working booms and fishing sails were removed, her running gear was completely overhauled, and racing sails were bent on her topmasts.

Most of the fishermen would have preferred to race their boats in working garb, keeping everything aboard except salt and fish, for the elaborate preparations for the races were expensive. In a sense they defeated the purpose of the races, which, in theory at least, was to improve the whole industry's techniques of catching fish. The races didn't cause *them* to change their clothes, however, for the very good reason that most of them owned but one blue serge suit which was purchased when they got married and worn until they were laid out for burial. On board the vessel it was an old flannel shirt, a vest, an odorous pair

of pants, and black oilskins tied at the openings with bits of
twine. Some men had turn-brimmed oilskin hats, but for most, a
woolen cap sufficed. Underwear was an exceptional luxury;
woolen mittens were a matter of life and death. On dress-up
occasions like the races, the men wore what they always wore,
perhaps adding a derby for formality, like Elias Walter's old
cook. It was many years later that the turn-brimmed yellow hats
and coats came into general use. Yellow oilskins increased a

sailor's visibility on deck or, God forbid, in the water. But in the days of the first schooner races, a bright yellow get-up would have been hooted off the wharves as being fit only for sissies.

The first of three elimination races was scheduled for October 15. The winner of this series would represent Canada at the forthcoming races with the Americans. By eight o'clock that morning there was standing room only in and around Halifax harbor, for no one had forgotten last year's events. The hopes, the thrills, and the humiliations were as fresh and keen as yesterday. People saw themselves larger than life, saw the humdrum of their days expanded and made dramatic on a nine-mile-wide screen, and in this singular drama, every man, woman, and child could be his own hero. Everybody came to Halifax— housewives, clerks, school children, blacksmiths, farmers, carpenters, preachers, and gamblers. An enterprising printer ran off hundreds of copies of the four possible racing courses outlined by the racing committee, and for everyone present, wind velocity and direction became the most vital information he could possess.

The crowd went wild when *Bluenose* tripped into the harbor. Her decks sparkled under a fresh coat of varnish, her sails were snowy-white, and she looked for all the world like Cinderella dressed for the ball. But as if to spite her skipper, there was barely enough wind to blow a paper across a puddle. The committees conferred, postponed, muttered, and prayed. The crewmen, most of them skippers themselves, fussed about, securing a second time knots which had been perfectly tied the first. One or two, standing at a safe distance from the crowd on deck, even dared to whistle softly in the hope of bringing on the wind. With his customary self-control, Angus limited himself to a few unprintable phrases, ending with an appeal to the sky to "fetch up a liddle blow." He'd no more have whistled aboard a vessel than he'd have worn yellow mittens or spoken the word "pig" aloud or left a hatch cover upside down, for anyone in his right mind knew that such carelessness would surely bring a Jonah aboard. There was enough bad luck wandering about the fishing fleet on its own, without anyone's courting it through sheer stupidity.

Two hours after the official starting time, the eight vessels and the crowds watching them were still shifting nervously about, skippers awaiting the signal to line up. At last the sharp report of a small gun brought the boats into position—well behind the starting line, for their sails were set, and if they crossed the line too soon, they would have to turn around and go back.

At that, there was a full four-minute difference in positions when the cannon signaled the start, with *Bluenose* out in front and last year's winner, *Delawana*, bringing up the rear. Between them ran *Independence, Canadia, Alcala, J. Duffy, Ada R. Corkum,* and *Donald J. Cook.*

The seven-and-a-half knot breeze made the start of the race look more like a gaggle of girls skipping along at a Sunday School picnic than racehorses breaking from the barrier. Exasperated, each skipper pushed his vessel along as best he could, spilling not a drop of available wind. By the time they reached the first marker, Inner Automatic Buoy, six miles south of the starting line in Halifax harbor, the weather began to yield to collective entreaty. The wind freshened to twelve knots, and it began to look as if there would be a real race after all. *Bluenose* turned the first corner four minutes ahead of *Canadia* and nine minutes ahead of *Alcala.* Then fog off Chebucto Head shut all the vessels out of sight, but the pace of the schooners never slackened. It was blowing fifteen knots by the time they reached the third lap, a windward thrash of nine and a half miles to the Sambro Lightship, and a twenty-mile wind was waiting for them at the mouth of Halifax harbor. *Bluenose* was "a perfect witch to windward." Less than three minutes had separated the three front runners at the halfway mark, but *Bluenose* crossed the finish line four minutes ahead of *Canadia* and seven in front of *Alcala. Cheers! Cheers! Cheers!*

The second race, on October 17, proved that someone had been listening when some rash and foolish fellow had whistled up the wind, for the day came in with a twenty-five-mile-an-hour blow, two knots higher than the velocity which had frightened the New York Yacht Club into postponing its races two years before. "This is more like it!" everybody said as the wind shrieked in the shrouds and made everyone in Halifax a "Bluenose" in the flesh.

The race started out tense, and at the halfway mark *Delawana* actually darted ahead of *Bluenose,* but when the schooners came on the wind, *Bluenose* tore ahead like driven smoke. Like her skipper, she required a lot of opposition to bring out the best in her. The harder he worked her, the better her spirit. The shouts of men could scarcely be heard above the cries of working timbers, the creak of straining sheets, and the anvil blows of her blue-black hull against the water. She crossed the finish line more than sixteen minutes ahead of the runner-up, *Delawana,* and established beyond a doubt her right to represent Canada.

But south of the border, a very nasty argument was brewing. Even before the sinking of the American trophy winner, *Esperanto,* the shipbuilders of Massachusetts had decided to better their best by building a new boat. It was no secret down in Gloucester that the Canadians were spending lavishly to make *Bluenose* a winner, but when it came to lavish spending, no one could compete with the Americans.

A group of Boston builders, suppliers, and yacht people got together and hired W. Starling Burgess, the famous yacht designer, to build them a vessel which, though a saltbanker, would be the speediest thing under sail. The name of their vessel was to be *Mayflower,* and she came off the ways at Essex a raving beauty by any man's standard.

But some miles north of Boston, the Gloucester fishermen began to boil. *"Mayflower's* not a genuine saltbanker!" they declared. "She's a gentleman's yacht, tricked out in a working vessel's disguise!" In spite of the clamor, her Boston owners insisted on their rights and sent *Mayflower* out to the Banks to put in her qualifying summer of work. She sailed under Capt. Harry Larkin, a fine skipper and an excellent fisherman, but she made only a modest showing at the scales when she returned to Gloucester with her catch. "She's a fresh fisherman, not a saltbanker!" claimed the Gloucestermen. "If you enter that blasted yacht as the American choice, you fellows on the racing committee can forget to call us out to see your rotten race!"

If the American fishermen in Gloucester were roiled, their Canadian counterparts were smoking at the ears. "If they enter *Mayflower,* our vessels will stay at the wharf. We're not going to have those slick Yankees turn this race into another farce, like the America's Cup Races" was the consensus in Lunenburg.

A representative of the American committee ran up to Halifax to speak for *Mayflower,* and a representative of the Canadian committee ran down to Boston to look over the controversial contender. In fact, the chairman of the Canadian committee, a prominent merchant and amateur yachtsman by the name of H. R. Silver, went down to the shipyards in Essex to watch *Mayflower's* launching. Some say Silver had had even more to do with the building of *Bluenose* than any other man in Nova Scotia—more, even, than Sen. William Dennis—and certainly H. R. Silver wanted as much as any other Canadian to see *Bluenose* win. But in his own mind he could find no fair reason to disqualify *Mayflower.* If her cost had been unusually high, the same thing could be said of the Canadian entry. It was only a matter of degree. But Angus, who was a good friend of "H.R.'s" under ordinary circumstances, was utterly exasperated with him and with all the Halifax men who were supposed to defend Canadian interests. "Those fellas on the committee would give in to the Yankees on anything, no matter how crazy. I had to spend most of my time either fightin' them or tryin' to put some stiffenin' in their backbones!" he said quite some time later.

The wrangle over the Boston vessel grew, and it began to look as if the International Fishermen's Races were going to be over before they had really begun. Perhaps it was a mercy when some sharp-eyed fellow noted in public that *Mayflower's* waterline was one foot longer than the legal 112-foot limit. It was like saying that the princess could not attend the ball because her belt was too big or her garter too tight. But it served the purpose. The pampered darling of the Essex shipyards was disqualified.

With *Mayflower* out of the picture, for the time being at least, the Gloucestermen got ready to give it another go. They held a speedy elimination race and the winner was the schooner *Elsie,* the same boat which had rescued the crew of *Esperanto* off Sable Island a few months before. At *Elsie's* helm would be the same Capt. Marty Welch who had sailed *Esperanto* to victory in the first year of the races.

Nova Scotians knew and respected Marty Welch, and they gave him a truly great reception when he sailed into Halifax. *Elsie*'s crew, like *Bluenose*'s, was composed almost entirely of skippers, and the welcome the Nova Scotians laid on for the Gloucestermen was as hearty and as generous as their far-famed hospitality could make it.

If the racing fever had been high at the elimination trials, there was near pandemonium as *Bluenose* met *Elsie* at the starting line. Tacked to her sails and driven into her hull were the hopes of all Canadians for the redemption of their national honor. For the Gloucestermen, their representation by *Elsie* was a triumph over the scheming financial manipulators of their home state of Massachusetts. *Elsie* was an old girl, but she had plenty of zip left in her stout timbers.

Yet this day, too, was not to pass without its torments. Angus had taken *Bluenose* back to Smith & Rhuland to be reexamined before the big race. He was bustling back from Lunenburg to Halifax with his beauty, and he surveyed the sea with narrowed eyes. He had much company on the water. Every barge and skiff, every tramp steamer and naval vessel and rowboat, every raft had poked its nose out of port for a look at the Canadian entry. As Angus skimmed past Pennant Buoy, who should turn up on his weather but that brazen American hussy, *Mayflower*! What gall, poking her impudent nose into this respectable company!

This brief encounter of two great vessels, both on the way to Halifax, is as good a place as any to look at the odd way in which some small event in real life becomes "history." Twenty-five years after this meeting, two books were published about the schooner races. One was by a Canadian, who wrote of it in these words: "*Mayflower* decided to give her [*Bluenose*] a brush. *Mayflower* fell behind consistently on this point of sailing, which was not the Lunenburger's best, but it was evident the Boston schooner was not being pushed and the brush was not regarded, of course, as settling the respective merits of the two schooners."

But an American writer described it this way: "To revenge herself on the *Bluenose*, the *Mayflower* went over the racecourse that year, and her manner of outsailing the *Bluenose* was scandalous to view."

At first view, the American's statement looks just as believable as the Canadian's, but it must be remembered that conditions on the racing course changed from moment to moment. If *Mayflower* had sailed the course alone, she might have done it faster than either vessel in the official race, or so the writer implies, but such a record would be meaningless unless the vessels raced simultaneously. Although the American writer was convinced of *Mayflower*'s superiority, *Bluenose* outsailed her the only time they met on equal terms.

Forty years later, there were still arguments about it in the columns of the *Halifax Herald.*

Had Angus Walters and Harry Larkin got together and drawn up a set of racing rules that both would abide by, there would have been no bitterness, no matter which man won. But a race between *Bluenose* and *Mayflower,* had it ever been held, would have been between two prima donnas, an expensive boat versus a lavish one, both designed with an eye on the races by men who were basically yacht designers. Even the most partisan person would have had to concede that the purpose of the Fishermen's Races would have been utterly defeated by it.

Bluenose was considerably bigger than the American defender, *Elsie.* The Canadian vessel was twenty-one feet longer, two feet wider, two feet deeper, and carried 2000 more square feet of sail. On the other hand, the Gloucester vessel was the descendant of nearly a century of boatbuilding for speed, and her overall size would not, by itself, have made her slower. It was no surprise, then, that the race was nip and tuck.

First one vessel shot ahead, then the other. A keen wind of twenty-five knots was blowing from the start, and when they reached the next to last marker, the two vessels were only seconds apart. Then *Elsie*'s fore-topmast carried away. Gallantly, Angus immediately doused his own ballooner and finished that lap with less sail than *Elsie* carried. By the last marker the wind had increased to a wild twenty-seven knots. It was then that Angus gave his charge her head. *Elsie*'s owner, a seasoned salt with forty years on the Banks behind him, jumped up and down on the
52

deck of the press boat as he watched his vessel drop steadily behind. "Poor little *Elsie!* My poor little *Elsie!*" he cried. *Bluenose* galloped home with her scuppers awash, a full thirteen minutes ahead of the Gloucesterman, having maintained an average speed of eleven knots on the forty-mile course. Sure enough, she was a record breaker!

Two days later, on October 24, 1921, the second race was held. This was the contest which would decide whether the trophy stayed in the States or came home to Lunenburg, where every loyal Nova Scotian believed it belonged. Two noncontenders turned up on the course: *Mayflower* again and *Delawana*, the Canadian vessel which had lost the previous year to the Americans. They gave each other a hook, and *Delawana* routed the Boston boat, but *Mayflower* was sailing only under her four lowers, without her racing rig, so again the race proved nothing but someone's intention to rattle the real contestants.

Once again *Elsie* held her own against *Bluenose* right up to the last lap. But when it came to working to windward, nothing seemed to be able to beat the Canadian. On the twelve-and-a-half-mile stretch from the Outer Automatic Buoy to the finish line, *Bluenose* picked up any time she might have lost on the way round, and she reached the finish line three miles ahead.

As fast as radio could carry it, the news flashed across the great sprawling northland. In sod cabins on the prairies and high in the Rockies, the word went out: "We've won! We've beaten the Americans!" Canada had fashioned a heroine out of its very own fiber, and the whole country took her to its heart.

Halifax was a happy harbor that night. Aboard *Bluenose* the hardcase skippers stamped around, pounding each other on the back. A big wooden crate was carried down to the fo'c'sle, and the mate called for a hammer to pry the lid loose. Inside stood twelve bottles of vintage champagne, with a note of congratulations from the owner of *Elsie*. Everyone aboard took a sip, holding out a stubby pinkie, as befitted the delicate taste of the bubbly wine. But these were saltwater men, and champagne was for yachting parties.

"To hell vit diss apple chuice!" cried one of the Lunenburgers. "Break out de rum!"

Chapter Seven

The Fishermen's International Competition had attracted far more attention than their most enthusiastic backers had hoped for, overshadowing even the America's Cup Races that year. Like any other great sport contest, it drew publicists, newspapermen, gamblers, yacht people, and professional flag-wavers like flies to honey. Quite apart from the prize money involved, a lot of private money changed hands, and people tended to put their mouths where their money was. A lot of the noise was made not for the men who laid their lives on the line every time they made a trip to the Banks, but for the good times the races provided to anyone with five dollars to spend.

Nothing was being proved about the efficiency of fishing vessels. In 1920 the big Canadian *Delawana* had taken a beating from the smaller U. S. *Esperanto*. The next year the bigger *Bluenose* had galloped away from the smaller *Elsie*. While the two races canceled out any possible conclusion on the relation of size to speed, no one asked whether a big schooner with a larger carrying capacity was really more economical to operate than a smaller one, nor whether the maximum size of sail had actually been reached with the 4000 square feet of canvas carried on *Bluenose*'s 86-foot main boom. In the welter of talk about timing and sailing style, no one asked the one question that everyone should have been asking: Did wooden sailing schooners of any size have a future in the face of the increasing number of steam-powered steel trawlers which were appearing on the Banks?

It might have been asked, too, whether deck engines instead of muscle power could not be used to hoist sail and anchors, and to pump water out of the hull. Wooden vessels were not watertight, and in heavy seas the vessel's chances for survival were measured by the number of strokes on the hand pump per hour required to keep her floating. "She was leaking 300 strokes per hour" meant a vessel was in bad shape, and the danger was compounded by crystallized salt in the pipes, which could block the pumps and sink the ship. Would not the installation of electrically powered pumps increase the safety of the fleet? Here, surely, was a legitimate question, but it was never raised. The introduction of electricity could have provided light belowdecks —and even heat whereby a fisherman might dry out his clothing instead of wearing it half-wet to drenched most of the time he was away at sea. Could not a better and safer way of catching fish be found than by sending men out in tiny boats and leaving them defenceless against the sea? In all the concern for efficiency someone might even have inquired how a fisherman was supposed to support a family on an annual income which was often less than $500 a year. In newspaper offices and in sporting circles, such questions would have been in very bad taste, for they would have spoiled the fun and games. But there wasn't a kitchen in Nova Scotia in which they were not discussed, and hotly too.

Next to the oxen, the women probably worked the hardest, the average lifetime career of a fisherman's wife being "to split fish and bear children." In addition to running the farms, they mended clothes, made soap, harvested hay and potatoes, raised children, and in many towns along the coast tended the flakes as well.

In those days a good part of the Lunenburg fleet tied up at the wharf for the winter. Men repaired gear, painted the boats, and traded yarns. Those owners who could afford a second set of gear refitted their schooners for the freighting trade, carrying salt fish and lumber to the West Indies and Europe, and bringing back rum, molasses, and salt. But there was much to do, even for the men who stayed at home. A good many fishermen were part-time farmers. Before they left for the spring trip to the Banks, they plowed their fields and left their wives and children

55

I had many a backache at the old hand pumps on a/of schooner in 1920 & 1921 to 1925 or so.

to tend the crops while they were out to sea. Until the 1940s there were more horses in Nova Scotia than there were cars or trucks, and along the fishermen's coast there were more oxen than there were horses. The slow old-country beasts were the gasoline engines of their time. They hauled logs out of the woods and plowed the fields; they stood patiently upon the frozen inland lakes while farmer-fishermen cut great square chunks of ice from the surface, then hauled them on sleds to the icehouse for use aboard ship. Oxen worked at the wharves until 1956, not only in transporting salt, fish, and other cargo, but in hoisting gear on the vessels anchored alongside.

Salt fish had to be spread out and turned for four or five days before it was cured. If fog came in, or rain, all the fish had to be gathered at once and placed under cover. A soft cure, after only a day or two in the sun, produced "wet fish."

A well-dried codfish was a pretty sturdy bit of hardware. Henry Thoreau, the great American philosopher, wrote in his beautiful book *Walden:*

"Who has not seen a salt fish, thoroughly cured for this world, so that nothing can spoil it, and putting the perseverance of the saints to the blush? with which you may sweep or pave the streets, and split your kindlings, and the teamster shelter himself and his lading against sun, wind, and rain behind it,—and the trader, as a Concord trader once did, hang it up by his door for a sign when he commences business, until at last his oldest customer cannot tell surely whether it be animal, vegetable, or mineral, and yet it shall be as pure as a snowflake, and if it be put into a pot and boiled, will come out an excellent dunfish for a Saturday's dinner."

Today the flakes are gone, and from the coastal road which winds around the Nova Scotian shore, Lunenburg looks like a sleepy little village, its deep harbor indistinguishable from the thousands of inlets and bays of the oceanfront. But Lunenburg had its great moment in history. Between 1880 and 1930 it was one of the most important ports on the whole North Atlantic coast.

Lunenburg was settled by the ancestors of its present population in 1752 and 1753. They came in two shiploads, mostly from inland parts of Germany and France, and very few of them knew anything about fishing. They were imported to Nova Scotia by the British rulers of Halifax for reasons which do not seem quite so honorable today as they did two hundred years ago. Having driven the French settlers from their homes and farms during the great expulsion of the Acadians, the English wanted pro-English Protestants living on Halifax's southern flank, lest the French muster their scattered forces and return to reclaim what had once been theirs.

Of course, the French had expelled the Micmac Indians a hundred years earlier, and of course, the land, if it belonged to anyone, really belonged to the Indians. The Micmac may well have been the best seamen of any of the human inhabitants of Nova Scotia, for they were able to navigate their fragile canoes across the wide and treacherous waters separating Nova Scotia from Cape Race, in Newfoundland, to trade with the now extinct Beothuk Indians. In 1911, at the first Fishermen's Regatta in Digby, Nova Scotia, several canoeloads of Micmac participated in the demonstrations, but they would not race. Such competitiveness was beneath their dignity. It was assumed that if a man was alive, he could handle his body with strength and agility, and that he would always do his best. And so they paddled along in peace, and puffed upon their pipes, while the white men made fools of themselves.

Perhaps it was significant that this regatta took place on the "French" Shore, which Longfellow made famous as the Acadia of his poem "Evangeline." Relations between the French and the Indians always seemed to be a little better than between the English and the Indians, or the English and the French. Relations could not have been perfect between the English and the Germans, else Lunenburg would not have kept to itself for a hundred and fifty years, to the point where a Lunenburger's speech is still distinguishable anywhere from the speech of anyone else in Nova Scotia. It is still a town dominated by names like Knickle, Zinck, Spindler, Rhodenziner, Himmelman. The shape of the windows of the town's finer houses is still distinctly German in character.

After their first big adventure of coming to the New World in search of land, the German settlers stayed put, stayed together, and worked hard. They were not the sort of people to rush into anything new. It was not until nearly thirty years after their arrival in the New World that they took to the trade that one day would make them famous. They had come, after all, as farmers. But Nova Scotian soil was poor, and the land was dense with forests—magnificent stands of hardwood. Just north of Lunenburg, there was a settlement of Yankees. Men of Chester concentrated on shipbuilding and the export of lumber, and their vessels were soon sailing halfway round the world. Lunenburgers learned from their neighbors, but they concentrated on building boats for the fishery at their doorstep, and their men became inshore fishermen. The first large vessel built in Lunenburg was produced in 1787, more than thirty years after the founding of the town. One hundred years later—when Ben Anderson went out to the Banks—they were still concentrating on fishing close to home. But in that century they had learned to build beautiful fishing boats.

58

In 1880 a tally of the vessels on the Grand Banks showed New England in the lead with 340 vessels. Newfoundland was close behind with 330, and Nova Scotia had 200, nearly all of them made in Lunenburg. In that year Nova Scotia ranked fourth among all the nations of the world in shipowning—seven hundred vessels flew her flag. Considering her small population, it seemed that in Nova Scotia, to be a man and to go to sea meant one and the same thing.

Lunenburg continued to hold her own in the salt-fish trade, even though it had fallen off a good deal before World War I. In 1914 there were 150 schooners in Lunenburg harbor, where once there had been 200. At the end of the war the fleet was down to 100 vessels. During the middle years of World War I it looked as if the whole of the fishing-fleet industry might be permanently destroyed. German submarines, hunting the warships and supply convoys that berthed at the Royal Naval Station at Halifax, suspected that many of the fishing boats along the coast were doubling as military vessels in disguise, and often they were correct. More than a third of the Lunenburg fleet was simply shot and sunk. The British Navy itself did inestimable damage to the schooner fleet as well, ramming into the wooden ships in the fog or at night, when even a schooner's riding lights had to be extinguished as a wartime safeguard.

Not all the vessels were lost because of direct hits or collision. Because of the danger of attack, Banks fishing was abandoned altogether and the fishermen hugged the coast. When a sudden squall blew up close to shore, the saltbankers had no room for maneuver, and many were driven up on the rocks before they could alter tack and head out to the relative safety of the open sea.

Sometimes two fishing vessels collided. The story is told of a saltbanker whose crew had gone below to dry out and take a snooze after a terrible dousing. Along came a steel steamer and sliced her in two. The crew scrambled to the after half of their ship to mount the rope ladder onto the steamer's deck while the forward half gurgled under. The last man to mount the ladder had been trying to dry out his clothes behind the galley stove. He climbed the rope ladder, stark naked, descended the companionway of the steamer, and resumed his nap in someone else's bunk. It was a rare collision which had so happy an ending. In Kipling's classic story of the Grand Banks, "Captains Courageous," we read about a collision with another sort of outcome. Indeed, just such an accident occurred during the very writing of this book. There were only three survivors to describe the hit-and-run disaster in which a wooden fishing vessel was abandoned after being splintered by a steamer just off the coast of England.

The shipbuilding boom which struck Nova Scotia right after World War I had a relatively short life. One hundred fourteen wooden vessels were built in 1919, many of them three-masted, or tern, schooners for the carrying trade, but by the following year the pace had begun to slacken.

When *Bluenose* won the international competition in October, 1921, there was still enough confidence in the wooden schooner for other vessels to be built in the hope of beating her. A group of Canadians on the South Shore built for that very purpose a vessel called *Mahaska*. Down in Massachusetts, the Yankees were determined to win the trophy again. W. Starling Burgess, whose disqualified *Mayflower* rankled in the hearts of her countrymen, was engaged to design another contender for the races. She was the *Puritan*—and "a ghost on the water." She did fifteen knots without trying and often averaged runs of fourteen and a half. She was the first Gloucester boat to have radio receiving aboard, and she was launched with great fanfare on March 25, 1922.

On her maiden trip she fell in with *Mayflower*, off Cape Cod, and gave her a solid trouncing. She made two halibuting trips, and was on her way to a third when she struck the northwest bar of Sable Island. The speed that made her great had led to her ruin. She had overrun her course by twenty miles. Gordon W. Thomas, in his *"Fast and Able": Life Stories of Great Gloucester Fishing Vessels* (Historic Ships Associates, 1968) describes what followed:

> "Heavy seas were breaking over her and there was a mad scramble to leave the vessel. The first dory capsized and one man drowned. Fifteen of the crew got away in dories and headed for the Nova Scotian coast. Captain Jeffrey F. Thomas and the seven

remaining members decided to make for Sable Island. The skipper and Israel Larkin jumped into a dory. A breaker carried the dory up on the rail of the vessel and the deck wash swept the skipper overboard. Fortunately another wave swept him back. Captain Thomas and Larkin finally succeeded in getting their dory clear and they joined the other two dories that had left ahead of them. The fifteen who had headed for Nova Scotia were picked up after they had rowed fifty miles by the LaHave schooner *Coral Spray* (a Nova Scotia vessel)."

Between March 24 and June 24 of the year 1922, *Puritan* had experienced all she would ever know about life and death.

The loss of *Puritan* was a severe blow to American hopes for victory in the upcoming races in October, but another vessel built down in Essex, Massachusetts, and named *Henry Ford* was groomed to hook with *Bluenose*. The owners of *Mayflower* had not given up their position either, and the talk of all the salt-bankers that summer turned inevitably to the coming contest.

Only the very solemn and sophisticated men of the Northeastern coast—the lawyers, the legislators, the chairmen of corporations, and the like—spent any time pondering the long-term effects on the fishing industry of a ruling announced at that time by the U. S. Supreme Court, charging the Boston Fish Pier, which operated a fleet of steam trawlers, with conspiring to monopolize the market by buying up twenty-five independent companies. Would this decision lengthen the life-span of the schoonermen and keep the small independent operators in business? Would it hamper the development of more efficient processing and distribution of fish? Would the coastal towns be better off or worse because of it? These were questions that were much harder to answer than whether Americans or Canadians built faster fishing vessels, and because they were so much harder to answer, very few fishermen on either side of the border even tried.

To the men who lived their lives on the slippery decks of schooners, or off in dories on the open sea, or waiting with their white, bloated hands hanging at their sides while the catch was weighed and the shares were calculated, the schooner races were a diversion and a relief.

Bluenose put in a fine season on the Banks that year. Her

hold was so full of fish that "they were nailin' cod to the masts!" And then it was the end of summer, and the fleet came home. A college girl described the scene in Lunenburg:

"This was the time of excitement and activity. Boats plying to and from the schooners discharging cargoes, taking in supplies or getting the vessels cleaned and painted before they are laid up for the winter. There is nothing more beautiful than to see a vessel in calm weather, with all her sails spread, moving grandly, almost pompously along toward the sea. Or if there is a high wind and the harbor is rough and choppy to see her come hurrying around Battery Point and into the harbor, sails all spread with flag flying. The fish was unloaded, the vessels scrubbed down and the fun began."

At the first elimination trials, held on October 7, 1922, *Bluenose* defeated three contenders, crossing the line five minutes ahead of her closest rival. *Mahaska,* built to beat her, trailed *Bluenose* over the finish line twenty minutes later than the champion. Her captain expressed his rage by jumping on his derby.

Down in Gloucester, the handsome *Henry Ford,* which had been damaged shortly after her launching, was back in shape again and was scheduled for a runoff against *Elizabeth Howard* and *L. A. Dunton.* The day before the runoff, the three vessels were engaged in a practice spin when along came the pride of Boston, the schooner *Mayflower.* Aboard that day was the Canadian newspaperman Frederick W. Wallace, who reported that some of the owners of *Mayflower* urged Captain Larkin to swing after the "legitimate" racers, and swing after them he did.

Wallace wrote: *"Mayflower* shot into the wake of the *Ford.* The breeze was fresh and the vessel with all her kites aloft went boiling along with scuppers awash and her lee rail dripping. We came up on *Henry Ford* like driven smoke and sailed under lee in a fashion that left no doubt in the minds of any that the *Mayflower* was a clipper. While we were pacing the other craft and beginning to haul ahead of her, the cooler heads aboard began exhorting Larkin to quit. 'Swing off, skipper! For the love of Mike, swing off! If they see what this one can do, they won't give you a chance to race tomorrow!' But it was too late. The American Committee ruled her out on the grounds that she was a fresh fisherman and not a salt fisherman."

When Angus Walters pulled into Gloucester for the big races against *Henry Ford* a week later, he could hardly help taking a long close look at *Mayflower,* for she was anchored at a nearby wharf. "Why, they've bent every bloody bedsheet in Boston on her!" he exclaimed. In politer terms, Angus was saying that in his opinion the American vessels in general and *Mayflower* in particular carried too much sail for their size, and this explained the fact that in general, American vessels did better in light breezes than in stormy weather. *Mayflower* put in eighteen hard seasons of work catching cod on the Grand Banks, but she was never admitted to the races. Nearly forty years after her final banishment from the Fishermen's International Competition, the controversy flared up again as to whether *Bluenose* could have beaten her in a fair race or not. To his dying day, no one regretted the lost opportunity more than Angus Walters himself.

Feelings were running high down in Gloucester. The Americans felt they were having a bad time of it. Both their champions, *Esperanto* and *Puritan,* had been vanquished by the sea. *Mayflower* was barred from trying for the trophy. Now they had *Henry Ford,* a fine-lined schooner sailing under Capt. Clayton Morrisey, as good a saltwater skipper as ever held a wheel. But *Ford* was an uncertain bet. She had been badly damaged at her launching. Though the damage had been repaired, she added up to a big question mark. A lot of rough language flew about the docks between the Americans and the Canadians, and there was no one to pour any oil on the troubled waters, for everyone had a stake in the outcome. Even the wind refused to blow.

The first race was a limp affair. *Ford* beat *Bluenose* handily, but both vessels exceeded the six-hour limit and there was so little breeze that the racing committee declared that it was no race. Walters was in a rage with the committee. "Clayt won, and that's all there is to it!" he stormed. Both he and Morrisey threatened the committee that they would leave unless the race was allowed to stand. The committee went down to the docks in a body and made a fervent appeal to the patriotism of both crews. At last they relented and consented to give it another try, but the outcome was no better the second time. Angus and Clayton were standing at the rails of their two schooners, chatting amiably enough, when one of them said to the other, "Well, how about it? Sniff a breeze? What do you say we start?" They agreed on the spot and set about at once, several minutes before the men on the committee had inserted the blank cartridge in the gun which was to signal the official start of the race. *Ford* beat *Bluenose* by two and one half minutes this time, but once again the committee insisted that it was not legal.

The replies of both crews must be censored, but Angus finally prevailed, and the second race was officially given to *Ford*. By the third day the wind had picked up and *Bluenose* won. The contest rules required two wins out of three, and to that point neither vessel had a clear claim to victory.

By this time tempers were as taut as tight ropes.

The fourth and last race was sailed in a twenty-five-knot wind, and *Bluenose* pulled over the line six minutes ahead of the American challenger. *Bluenose* would take the trophy home to Canada.

The Ford would not stand up w
Heavy weather racing. Tender

But one of her crew would not be at his post. Boodle Demone, nephew of Angus Walters, was found drowned alongside the Gloucester dock. Fell in? Pushed off the dock in the dark of night? What was the reason for his death, anyway? No one really knew. Nothing could be proved. Young Boodle was just lying face down in the water when they found him, and he could not tell any tales.

All the heart went out of the game then.

Bluenose sailed back to Lunenburg carrying the silver trophy, but it was filled to the brim with bitterness.

Chapter Eight

Another winter passed, and once again the whine of saws and the thud of hammers driving treenails (trunnels) into hardwood could be heard along the shore. At Mahone Bay, a few miles north of Lunenburg, a new vessel, *Keno,* was launched and the talk was that she would beat *Bluenose*. But *Keno* was never to have a chance to prove her mettle. She set out in a heavy blow on her maiden voyage, bound for Newfoundland to pick up bait. Capt. Albert Himmelman put in at Louisbourg and reported his new vessel was handling well, but once she left Louisbourg, neither she nor any member of her crew was ever heard from again.

In the same month that *Keno* was presumed lost, the Story shipyards down in Essex, Massachusetts, launched a vessel which was financed by the same men who had commissioned *Puritan* the year before. Her name was *Columbia,* and by all accounts on both sides of the border, she was one of the most beautiful vessels ever built. "To see her sail," wrote J. B. Connolly in the foreword to *American Fisherman* by Albert C. Church, "coming bow on in a smooth sea and a fresh breeze—to see her so, viewing her from under her lee bow, and the way she had of easing that bow in and out of the sea—well, the beautiful lady was Poetry herself, then."

Columbia was smaller than *Bluenose,* but she was as fast as she was lovely to look at. Yet neither speed nor looks could overcome the awful Jonah some said lay hidden within her.

66

She made one fine trip and was outward bound for another when, off Sable Island, she was rammed by a steam trawler. Her forerigging was carried away and her bowsprit and rails were smashed. Although she was unable to complete her qualifying season, the racing committee agreed to allow her to enter the elimination trials late in October, when the damage to her forward end had been repaired. She raced against *Henry Ford* and *Elizabeth Howard,* but it was hardly a contest, for the outcome was clear from the opening gun. *Columbia* ran the course miles in front of the competition.

Now the Americans were certain that they had a contender to bring the trophy down to Gloucester and keep it there. *Columbia* left home amid the cheers of her well-wishers to take on the big Canadian. Outside her home port she struck a ledge of rock and had to return to the same repair dock which had just discharged her. The damage was not severe this time, and in a few days she was ready to race.

If there was any malice lingering in Halifax over the previous year's race, it was not in evidence when *Columbia* swung into the harbor. "The Gem of the Ocean" got a royal reception from her hosts. For Angus Walters, it was a long-awaited chance to race against his close friend and longtime rival, Ben Pine. Ben was one of *Columbia*'s owners and not her regular skipper, but like Marty Welch, he was one of the best in the Gloucester fleet. Like two champions meeting in the ring, the men shook hands and vowed to give each other no quarter when the race was run—and they didn't.

Bowsprit to bowsprit they battled around the course. Every second counted. On the third lap an incident occurred which ultimately ground the whole of fishing-schooner racing to a standstill. In essence, what happened was that Ben Pine crowded *Bluenose* so close to a reef that she escaped destruction or collision only by grazing *Columbia*'s shrouds. In the shock of contact *Bluenose*'s main boom was jarred from its jaws. It swung out and hooked on *Columbia*'s shrouds. Since *Bluenose* was in process of overtaking *Columbia* at the time, she actually towed the American boat for a minute and a half.

Here is the way the press reported it October 30, 1923:

Reports vary of the incident, but as near as can be gleaned the *Bluenose* was regaining the ground she had lost by overstanding and the *Columbia* kept luffing her. The vessels were bearing down on Bell Rock Buoy, with the *Bluenose* actually headed for the rock itself. The *Columbia* passed to leeward of the buoy—so close that she almost touched. The *Bluenose* had no choice; she was so far inshore and so near to danger that she was forced to pass between the buoy and the rock. By this time she had an overlap on the *Columbia*.

Bluenose's pilot shouted to her helmsman, telling him to keep off. The helmsman shouted back: "If I keep off I'll strike her." "You'll strike her on the rock, then," was the pilot's warning.

With the overlap complete, Captain Walters and the pilot both shouted for sea-room. The *Bluenose's* main-boom was broad off—and as the champion forged past the *Columbia,* her course altered to avoid the rock, the boom struck the challenger's main rigging. Then it struck her fore-rigging, hooking the sheer-pole and bending one end of it into a bow. She came clear here, only to strike again, this time at the jib-stay. At this point the *Bluenose's* mainboom hooked fast into the *Columbia's* jib down-haul. She towed the challenger in this position for close to a minute and a half. Then, she came clear and went into the lead . . .

It did not look then as though the *Bluenose* could win for the jolt of the fore sheerpole on her boom-end had unshipped that eighty-one foot spar from the saddle, and her mainsail was hanging like a broken wing. Seven of the *Bluenose* men laid hold of the huge 81-foot boom and by a superhuman effort lifted it back into place again.

The men of the *Bluenose* state that they did their best to bring her mainboom inboard in time to avoid striking the *Columbia;* but they could not. The rule in connection with this incident says:

BEAR →

"When a vessel is approaching a shore, rock, vessel or other dangerous obstruction, and cannot go clear by altering her course without fouling another vessel, then the latter shall, on being hailed by the former, at once give room; and in case one vessel is forced to tack or to beat away in order to give room, the other shall also tack or bear away as the case may be, at as near the same time as is possible without fouling. But if such obstruction is a designated mark of the course, a vessel forcing another to tack under the provisions of this section shall be disqualified."

68

In spite of the time lost in replacing the boom, a task ordinarily requiring eighteen men rather than the seven who accomplished it, *Bluenose* crossed the finish line one minute and thirty seconds ahead of *Columbia*. It was a clear win, and Angus did not need to reply when Ben Pine shouted across the water, "Never mind, Angus, I'll get you on the next one!"

That night the city buzzed with claims of foul and rumors of protests. Certainly Angus had grounds for complaint, for Ben could have been disqualified for his action under the existing rules. But Walters decided not to lodge a protest because, as he explained later, he had towed the challenger, and in spite of having been the puller-ahead rather than the pusher-behind, this could have been construed by a legalistic committee to be an infringement. Anyhow, *Bluenose* had covered the course a minute and a half faster than *Columbia,* and everybody had seen her do it, so why rub it in? Besides, there were two more races to come, in case anyone had lingering doubts.

The racing committee was alarmed, however, for if such maneuvers were permitted to escalate, a great sporting event could deteriorate into a cruel and tragic farce. Therefore the committee did the only thing a committee can do when faced by the excesses of human passion: It made another ruling, stating that all buoys were to be passed to seaward, thus guaranteeing that no vessel would rack up for want of sea room.

Both masters were notified by letter. Angus glanced at the memorandum, which he could only have interpreted as a warning from the committee to Ben, and laid it aside. Had he read it with the mind of a lawyer rather than with the mind of a skipper, he might have been spared considerable anguish.

The next day the committee called off a race in progress because the wind was too light. The two vessels finished the course unofficially and—unofficially—*Bluenose* won again. The following day blew in on a twenty-five-mile gale. This was *Bluenose* weather, and though *Columbia* tagged at her heels all the way, *Bluenose* still crossed the finish line two minutes and forty-five seconds earlier than the challenger.

Angus had good reason to grin. With two official wins out

of three, he'd won the series, and won it against the fastest and most able vessel the Americans could build.

But congratulations were not forthcoming. Instead he was informed that Ben Pine had lodged a protest against him for passing inside a customs buoy. To be sure, it *was* a buoy, but not one that marked a shoal. Obsolete for years, this particular bit of iron had been used as an inspection marker during World War I for cargo shipments out of Halifax. Walters hadn't shortened his course by choosing to pass it to port, and the buoy was not named as a marker in the sailing instructions. Nevertheless, the committee decided to award the race to Pine by forfeit.

Walters could scarcely believe his ears. "Make it no race," he offered, "but don't hand the race we won to the *Columbia* on a silver platter."

But the committee stood pat. There was talk of assembling a scratch crew to replace Angus's men. "Not on your life!" roared Angus when he heard of that plan. "Come on, boys, we're going home."

The committee had forgotten, apparently, that Walters owned the controlling share of the vessel, and they could not put him off his own ship. In consternation, the committee sent the Premier of Nova Scotia hurrying down to the wharf to plead with Angus, but to no avail. He cast off his lines and called for a tow into the wind. One by one the vessels in the area refused, for the racing committee had sent word to every ship in the harbor forbidding them to come to his assistance. Then an old coal scow with a Lunenburger at her helm came chugging by. "Hey, Joe, throw me a line!" bellowed Angus. Joe did.

Thus humbly escorted, *Bluenose* sailed out of Halifax, holding her head high, leaving the committee to try to figure out a way of carrying on the Fishermen's International Competition with only one contender. They summoned Pine and offered him the trophy. "No, thanks," he said, and sailed home empty-handed, no happier for all his trouble than *Bluenose* had been the year before.

The races were over, and they were going to remain over for a long, long time. *Bluenose* put her racing sails in mothballs and went back to salt fishing. For all its hardship, there was much

70

less heartache in fishing than there was in racing. A man did not expect the elements to be fair. A fisherman worked with the weather and the sea because they were the sources of his livelihood. When they turned against him, he fought for his life and for the life of his vessel with all the strength he had. If he won, he survived. If he lost, he perished. He might die for his lack of skill or luck or judgment, but he was never humiliated. Only men had the power to attack one another's honor.

⚓

Bluenose more than held her own in the fishing business, but she had plenty of stiff competition from the Lunenburg fleet. Vessels like *Vena P. Thornhill, Vivian Smith, Marguerite H. Smith, Daisy M. Mossman,* and Angus's old vessel, *Gilbert B. Walters,* might not have been as fast as *Bluenose,* but they caught a tremendous amount of fish—as much as a quarter of a million pounds in a single fare. Most of the time Angus took *Bluenose* to Western Bank, but in the year of the race with *Columbia,* he had gone as far as Grand Bank and had come home with 2700 quintals—more than 600,000 pounds—putting him near the top of the town for that trip. It was just as well to be out of the spotlight for a time, for the excitement produced by the schooner races was spurious and deceiving, and there was enough peril in the ordinary operation of a fishing schooner to satisfy the most adventurous of men.

Even when the weather was calm, death waited in the water. Russell Tanner, a big, ruddy-faced fisherman who still lives in Lunenburg, tells of a day when he was working on *Bluenose.* "I fell down from 70 feet aloft," he says. "I was taking up the forestaysail halyard, a whole coil of rope around my neck, when I took cramps in both legs and couldn't move. After a while my hands got so numb they just let go. On my way down I struck the light box and bounced overboard, coil of rope and all. The light box saved my life."

Jack Pardy, who spent seven years as a doryman on *Bluenose,* tells of his good friend Jerry Cleveland, a quiet sort of fellow, married but with no children. "We'd given a tow to a vessel out of Port Hawkesbury, and Jerry climbed out on the

bowsprit—you know, that's the part of a vessel we always called the "widowmaker"—to put a sleeve on one of the ropes, for it was chafin'. It was a t'ick o' fog, we was on Quero (Banquereau Bank), there was no wind, but it had been a hard mornin'. I had a feelin' somethin' was goin' to happen. Jerry was out there on the footropes, working with both hands, when all of a sudden he falls into the water. He was a wonderful swimmer now, Jerry was, not like most of the fishermen. Captain lowered a dory with two men in it, and they was close enough to grab Jerry by the hand when he goes down like a stone. Just like a stone."

Jack Pardy remembers another time when he never expected to see land again. *Bluenose* was anchored off a lee shore of Sable Island in April, 1926. The fishing was good, and the trawls had been in the water for two days. That morning the dorymen had been out once to underrun the trawl and had left the vessel a second time when it began to breeze up and snow. Walters called the dories in and took a reading from the heaving lead. Twenty-eight fathoms was barely enough for maneuvering that close to Sable Island. A hundred and fifty fathoms of anchor cable held *Bluenose* at her anchorage, and the way the wind was tossing her put a great strain on the vessel. It took an hour on the windlass to shorten her cable, and meanwhile the sea kept mounting. Walters let her come up on the wind, and sounded his depth again. Eleven fathoms!

At five-thirty that night, the grandfather of all seas struck. A mountain of solid green water broke the cable, smashed out fourteen stanchions, and carried away part of her rail and bulwarks. One more broadside blow could have splintered her. Only by facing her attacker, letting the seas pour over her decks, could she hope to survive. Angus lashed himself to the wheel, adding the iron of his own will to the rudder's endurance, and with a double-reefed foresail on his vessel he beat her out, tack for tack, trying to get around the treacherous hook of Sable Island. ". . . *Bluenose* kept heading up, biting her way into the gale. Don't know as any other vessel could have done it. All you could do was to keep her going and hang on. . . ."

Recalling that this was the worst storm he had ever witnessed on the Banks, Angus reproached himself for having an-

73

chored where he had in the first place. But the fishing had been good, and the catch meant badly needed cash. "Finally the wind hauled nor'westerly. It was luck for us, because it hauled enough so we could let it drive us back far enough outside to clear the south coast and get into the open," he concluded. *Bluenose* was fortunate to have escaped without the loss of life. Two other Lunenburg vessels went down with all hands in that very same storm.

In a storm at sea, it took enormous courage merely to cross the deck, yet men climbed into the rigging when they had to, and considered themselves safe when a streaming deck lay under their feet.

Not every man was equal to such strain. Some men simply broke down or became immobilized by the overwhelming odds which faced them. They went below and waited for death to carry them off. There were skippers who allowed their vessels to dash to pieces when the spirit went out of them and they could fight no more.

It is very hard for us nowadays to conceive of the weight of a skipper's responsibility, for no modern machine, no matter how powerful it may be, puts as much control into one man's hands as the schooner placed in the hands of the skipper. The energy, the will, the judgments were all his. Nothing was shared with the private chemistry of a gasoline engine. The vessel was an extension of the skipper's bone and sinew; the hazards of the sea were a test of his personal character. The schooner was the agency through which an ordinary man might become a superman. Small wonder, then, that the love which often bloomed between a master and his vessel could be as deep and abiding as the love of a man for a woman. And that was the way it was between Angus Walters and *Bluenose*. "She never let me down," he used to say.

The damage wrought by the April storm was repaired in time for *Bluenose* to put in a hard summer on the Banks. There was no international race to look forward to, but there was a lot of fish to be caught. Jack Pardy still smiles when he remembers that lucky year. *Bluenose* brought home a record fare of 2936 quintals—646,000 pounds—of fish and every member of her crew was paid $336 as his share. Pardy bought his wife a new sweater after that trip.

Although it seemed that the international races were over for all time, still the sporting blood of the saltbank fleet ran hot on both sides of the border. Though reason could not justify such an investment, another group of Halifax men got together and commissioned William Roue to build a new vessel that would beat *Bluenose*. But she was a misbegotten creature from the start, and *Bluenose* ran her off the course in the very first race. "Stick a bowsprit in the Haligonian's stern and sail her stern first she'd do better" was Walters's appraisal of his so-called competition.

Meanwhile, down in Gloucester, *Columbia* was beating everything in sight, and a lot of people wondered what would have come of it if *Bluenose* and the lovely American had actually finished their series. The two vessels often met out on the Banks, but never to race.

On August 24, 1927, the entire American and Canadian fleets were out, finishing the last of their summer's trip. It was still too early for skippers to ask themselves whether to risk the one last trip of the season which so often turned out to be the one last trip of a lifetime. Hurricanes often waited until late in September to tear up the coast. A hundred and fifteen miles southeast of Halifax, *Columbia* lay at anchor within signal distance of half a dozen vessels of the Canadian fleet when, without warning, a hundred-mile-an-hour wind ripped across the Banks. In that maelstrom of screaming wind and water, *Columbia* went down with twenty-two hands; *Sadie E. Knickle*, *Mahala*, *Sylvia Mosher*, *Clayton Walters*, *Uda A. Corkum*, and *Joyce M. Smith* sank with a total loss of eighty-five men, and the skipper of *Mayflower* was tossed overboard and drowned. No one knew if *Columbia* had collided with a Canadian in that storm, for there were no survivors. This was the worst disaster suffered by the North Atlantic fishing fleet in decades, and it marked the end of salt fishing for the port of Gloucester. Only a month earlier, *Columbia* had brought in a stupendous fare of 350,000 pounds of salt fish. It proved to be the last fare of salt fish caught by a Gloucester vessel and landed at a Gloucester wharf.

In Gloucester and in Lunenburg, there were mass memorial services. Choirs gathered in the town squares, the names of the lost men were read aloud, and the assemblies of mourners moved down to the wharves to the muffled beat of funeral drums. One hundred twenty wreaths were piled upon the deck of a waiting schooner, which bore the flowers to the Banks and scattered them upon the waters. On that sad day there were many fishermen who wondered whether the end had not come also for the saltbank schooner, whether the symbolic burial was not in some part also their own.

Yet the last had not been heard from *Columbia*. More than a year later, on New Year's Day, 1929, the Canadian beam trawler *Venosta* was dragging about forty miles southwest of Sable when her gear got entangled in a wreck. Gordon Thomas describes the encounter thus in his *Fast and Able* stories: "With her powerful engines and winches pulling the taut cables, there slowly emerged from the sea, like a phantom ship, two masts with no topmasts. Slowly the form of the vessel came into view, rolling and pitching but on an even keel. The crew of the trawler were in danger of having their sides battered by the wreck, but suddenly the cables holding the wreck snapped and she slowly sank from sight. While the vessel was afloat the powerful floodlights of the trawler were thrown on the derelict. An eerie sight greeted the watchers. No sign of humans could be seen. The vessel seemed in good condition, the major portion of her rigging intact, but no sign of a name could be made out. Rough seas prevented any attempt to keep her afloat to ascertain if any bodies were in the cabin. But all aboard seemed to think she was the *Columbia*. . . ."

Jonah had had the last word.

Chapter Nine

Almost ten years had passed since that blustery day in March, 1921, when *Bluenose* tasted salt water for the very first time. In those years she had caught thousands of tons of fish, more than enough to pay back all the money invested in her building, and with very considerable interest. She had earned the right to an honorable retirement. Because of her the silver trophy of the Fishermen's International Competition had remained in Canada. Her career was living proof that a wooden vessel of great size and carrying capacity could be faster than a smaller one, and as economical to run—if indeed the founders of the races had ever seriously wondered about that question in the first place.

By this time, though, the further improvement of the design of a wooden sail carrier was as much beside the point as a new design for a one-horse shay would have been after Henry Ford began producing the Model "A." By 1930, beam trawlers and draggers outnumbered the wood and sail fleet by a wide margin, and no matter how hard they worked, the dory carriers could not compete with the catches of steam-powered vessels. The best trawl line was a one-hook one-fish affair, while a beam trawler scooped hundreds of tons of fish out of the sea in a single, mechanized operation, all of it performed by men working in relative safety from the deck of a big, metal ship.

In the States, the Great Depression began officially with the stock-market crash of October, 1929. Stockbrokers were leaping out of Wall Street office windows, bankruptcies were as commonplace as unemployed apple sellers, and an astonished and dismayed public discovered that the sand which had been thrown into the moneymaking machine was not an easy substance to remove.

Up in Nova Scotia, in one of the rare instances of things moving faster farther north than they did in the States, the depression had got an earlier start. The bottom seemed to have dropped out of the market for salt cod, and there were no takers, even with cod selling at six cents a pound. Brazil and the West Indies simply had no money with which to buy—at any price. The saltbank skippers and fish dealers began asking themselves how long they could keep going in the trade when the only market seemed to be in fresh or frozen fish. Nova Scotia lacked the processing plants and it lacked the refrigerated truck and rail transport to carry a fresh product to market. Ten days was the longest a catch would keep without salt, and the only way for skippers to reach a big center of population like Boston or New York was to sail to it. Distance alone put Nova Scotia at a terrible disadvantage with her American competitors. The only answer was to change the whole technique from the long saltbank trips to the short fast runs which the Americans had been making for three quarters of a century. Sail-powered vessels simply could not move fast enough, dependent as they were upon the whims of wind and weather, and vessels with a huge carrying capacity could not stay out long enough with a load of fresh fish to fill up their holds.

The industry had been in peril for some time, but the year 1930 was a very bad year. For *Bluenose* it was awful. In March, Angus had turned *Bluenose* over to his brother Sonny Walters, who took her up to Newfoundland to buy bait. Sonny took a Newfoundland pilot aboard to help him navigate into the safe, ice-free port at Placentia Bay, where he hoped to buy herring. By following the pilot's directions, Sonny fetched his charge up on a Newfoundland reef, forty miles away from hope of help. For four days *Bluenose* lay upon her side while sand and water seeped into her hull. First one tugboat tried to tow her off, then two, working together. She came free finally, and they took her to a Newfoundland yard for repairs, but the work was poorly done and she handled sluggishly.

Close to the summer's end, Ben Pine came up to Lunenburg with a proposition for Angus. Louis Thebaud, a wealthy French-Canadian who summered at Gloucester, had commissioned yet another vessel in the hope of besting *Bluenose*. She was equipped with engines, but she was a legitimate sail carrier, a trim little beauty named for his wife: *Gertrude L. Thebaud*. *Bluenose* was still the measure by which men judged sailing speed, and if *Thebaud* could not beat her, why, she just would not have proved herself and that was all there was to it.

"Naw, Ben," said Angus, shaking his head, "we're in no shape for a race. I can't afford to fool around with no races this year. Not makin' any money off fish, and you know what it would cost to put the old girl into racing trim. . . ."

"But, Angus, Sir Thomas Lipton will put up money for a cup, and there will be prize money. . . ." said Ben. "Come on, Angus, give it a go! Be a sport!"

"I'll send the wessel, but I won't go myself," said Walters, compromising.

"Then we don't want *Bluenose*," Ben replied.

"I'll think on it," was all that Angus would promise. But when the racing date rolled round that October, *Bluenose* was there in Gloucester, and Angus was standing at her wheel.

She had worked until the very last minute. Her sails were far too big and baggy, her keel had been badly repaired and she was "off course." She carried ten more tons of ballast on one side than she did on the other to compensate for all the sand she had sucked in on the Newfoundland coast, and she was a ten-year-old vessel up against a brand-new spring chicken, fresh out of the yards.

Thebaud skipped around the course in fifteen fewer minutes than *Bluenose*. From Boston to California the sportswriters of the United States got a crack at a front-page headline: CANADIAN CHAMPION DEFEATED BY AMERICAN!

The series wasn't over, but nothing better was to come of it for *Bluenose*. Walters's crew worked all night to cut yards off

Bluenose's sails. The next two races were called off because of light winds, and the fourth was well under way, with *Bluenose* far in the lead, when the committee—was there *ever* a decent committee?—called off the race, claiming that visibility was too poor for the skippers to see the marking buoys. The skippers, who had been seeing them well enough to be giving each other a fast and honest race, were simply exasperated.

Maybe this time Angus's anger and frustration turned inward upon him, for when the final race was held a few days later, it was he, and not *Bluenose,* who failed to meet the test. *Bluenose* was again running about five minutes in *Thebaud*'s lead, halfway through the course, when Angus split tacks. It was a fatal move, for he had maneuvered himself out of the wind. To his last day he could never understand what had made him use such poor judgment, but he never dodged the blame. *"Thebaud* didn't beat *Bluenose,* she beat *me!"* he insisted.

It was a hard blow to the Canadians, but they drew some consolation from the knowledge that the Lipton-sponsored race was not the one that really counted. Angus guessed that Ben Pine would not be long in pursuing him for big game, now that he'd accomplished what had seemed impossible. And he was correct. The following October, the two great skippers met once more at Halifax harbor to battle out the first Fishermen's International Competition to be held in eight years.

All Halifax turned out to see *Thebaud* run a challenge against their burly old queen. It was a two-race series. *Bluenose,* fully recovered now from the tribulations which had beset her the previous year, had never been in better form. To Ben Pine's immense chagrin, she took the first race by more than half an hour and the second by twelve minutes.

"The wood ain't growin' yet that'll beat *Bluenose!"* was one of Angus's favorite observations. And he had proved it once again on this very happy day.

The prize money from the 1931 series must have just about repaid the cost of putting the great Canadian back into fighting shape, but it was not enough to make much difference in anybody's pocketbook. Salt fishing was going from bad to worse. By 1932 the grim and hungry thirties had really dug in, tooth and talon, for what would soon seem like forever. Further racing, in the face of all that poverty and all that despair, now seemed just too frivolous an affair. For the men who haunted the wharves to escape the cry of hungry children, it was "Thanks for the Memory" so far as the schooner races were concerned.

It should not be supposed that the average fisherman in either Nova Scotia or Massachusetts had ever enjoyed what could be called prosperity, even during the halcyon Roaring Twenties. While fish dealers had been making unprecedented profits, and vessel owners were sometimes getting back eight to twelve thousand dollars on a twenty-thousand-dollar investment in a single year, the average fisherman was still earning between seven hundred and a thousand dollars a year. The prosperity of Lunenburg's upper class expressed itself on the streets of the upper town, which the twenties had lined with big, amply proportioned homes, solidly Germanic in character, filled with solid furniture, solid pantries, and solid morals. Solid bank accounts backed them up, for thrift and hard work were the fiber of the town, and rash or public spending would have been considered vulgar and "American" in the eyes of the town's "better people." Lunenburg had always reserved her praise for the men who stuck to their jobs and thought less about what they were paid than how well they did the work.

As jobs grew scarcer and the fear of chronic unemployment spread, ordinary fishermen had to push themselves to superhuman efforts merely to keep themselves and their families alive. By 1930 the average schooner was bringing in half a million pounds of fish a season, but the men who caught it were not earning enough to provide the barest necessities. Even the education of children became a luxury. Few went beyond the primary grades. Without education, there wasn't even any hope for the future.

Now the working populations began to lose their moorings. Newfoundland men moved down into Nova Scotia in search of work, and Nova Scotia men moved farther south into the States, where industry was more diversified, and if a man was not able to get a hitch on a fishing vessel, he could, with a lot of luck, find other work.

As the workingmen moved south, the machinery moved north, spreading from the States up the coast, replacing more and more men with iron winches and gigantic nets. Even in conservative Lunenburg, men could no longer afford to stay ashore during the winter, and the winter fishery became an accepted feature of life in the town, adding the burden of ice-choked rigging to the trials of the fishermen.

Walters remembered a three-month trip which netted him ten dollars. Another fisherman brought home $6.98 to his family as his season's pay. You couldn't give lobsters away in those days. "You made a penny and you sucked it for a week before you spent it," Angus said.

On most of the schooners deck engines had been installed by the end of the twenties, enabling a vessel to operate with even fewer than six men, but there were still some "hand pullers" about. There was no complaining about overwork in those days, no matter how weary and hard-driven a man might feel after sixty hours of continuous labor. A grumbler had only to hear the dread words "Put yer gear ashore!" to feel the hammer stroke of doom upon his heart. Some skippers, unable to meet their payrolls, made life so miserable for their crews that the men jumped ship, vanishing from sight without collecting their pay in what seemed a choice between slavery and starvation.

It seems inconceivable now that men went fishing in open dories in the months of December, January, and February, but thousands of them did. Even the steam-powered vessels were not safe during that time of year. In spite of their greater speed, these ships sometimes accumulated so much ice on their superstructures that they simply sank under the weight of it. Accidents aboard the steam trawlers might have been less frequent, but they were often more serious, particularly when overtired men were trapped and mangled by the heavy machinery.

By 1932 there were only about fifty schooners left on the Banks. They carried on a brave fight against the twin tides of misfortune and technological obsolescence, but their cause was without a future. One by one they surrendered to the times. Those owners who could afford to do so installed engines in their vessels. The others made less and less money with every passing year, until it became altogether uneconomical for them to sail their ships at all. Such schooners either rotted at the docks or went south to the West Indies to work for a pittance in the coastal freighting trade.

In the face of economic catastrophe, the old social order which had served so long and so well began to crumble. As mechanized vessels, manufactured for the most part in the States, began to move northward, the old way of hiring a man because you knew him, and could trust the quality of his work, began to change. Now a captain hired a man who was desperate enough to accept the wages and working conditions. Crews were drawn from a new population of floaters, constantly moving about in a search for jobs. Gone were the pride in the job, the loyalty to a captain or to a vessel. There wasn't even the comfort of working side by side with a man who sang next to you in the village choir, or to whose sons you gave your sweets when the vessel rolled into port. Men were strangers when they came aboard, and strangers when they departed. The boys weren't shoveling salt down on the wharves in the fervent hope of getting a chance to go out in a dory when they got a little older, or becoming fishermen—maybe captains if they were very, very good—for even salt-shoveling jobs were reserved for men with families to feed.

※

Down in the States, however, a new kind of camaraderie was coming into being. The American fleet had long been manned by first-generation Americans of Greek, Portuguese, Irish, Spanish, Italian, or French-Canadian ancestry. Few Negroes were employed, except as cooks, and the captains were likely to have been of Anglo-Saxon origin, but the men were accustomed to their ethnic differences and could overcome them enough to be able to think as a class and organize themselves into unions. There was a strong sense of social responsibility among the skippers too. In April, 1933, Ben Pine organized a large delegation of people active in the fishing industry, veteran fishermen as well as fish dealers, and sailed the *Gertrude L. Thebaud* down to Washington, D.C., to talk over the problems of the fishing industry with Pres. Franklin D. Roosevelt. The President himself went down to the pier to greet Captain Pine and his men, and promised to do whatever he could.

In Nova Scotia it was harder for people to get together. The very pride and self-reliance that made them such great fishermen prevented them from seeking each other's help in a common cause. Nova Scotia was still divided by towns, by traditions, by skills, by religions, and by nationalities. The Fundy Shore was separated from the South Shore not only by the fact that they built square-riggers and three- and four-masted schooners instead of two-masted vessels, and that they were involved in the fresh and inshore fisheries, but much more by the fact that they were poor, French, and Catholic. Lunenburg placed itself in a class apart because it built two-masted vessels, produced salt fish, and was 90% German, English, and Protestant. No one would admit it, but a Negro could never get a job on a saltbanker. The same discrimination which kept Frenchmen out of the Fishermen's International Competition also made it impossible for a Catholic to get work in the Lunenburg fleet.

Eventually all the counties in Nova Scotia introduced a system of cash allowances known as the dole. It was just enough money to keep people from starving to death. But there was no dole in Lunenburg. Lunenburgers ate herring and potatoes or they ate nothing at all, but they refused to stand in line to receive charity, not even from their own government. Nor did Lunenburg's men of wealth dig into their capital to meet the crisis. Throughout the depression Lunenburg had only one rival in all of Canada for the per capita deposits of money on deposit in her savings banks. That was Westmount, Quebec, the English-speaking enclave situated both physically and financially at the top of French-speaking Montreal. The depression which ravaged all of North and South America was especially hard on the fishing industry because it had always been a chancier business than others. In some ways neither New England nor Nova Scotia ever fully recovered from it.

Early in 1933 a large group of public people in the United States decided to organize a world's fair in the hope of injecting some life and confidence into a collapsed economy. They chose the city of Chicago as the site, for it was the heart of the con-

84

tinent's industry and agriculture. For the first time in her career *Bluenose* was to enjoy a small economic advantage from her status as a celebrity, for she was invited to represent Canada at the Chicago fair. A special corporation was formed to finance her journey up the St. Lawrence River and through the Great Lakes. *Thebaud* was invited to the fair too, and both vessels drew record crowds. It was worth twenty-five cents to a discouraged man to stand at the wheel of the anchored ship and imagine himself a hero, at least long enough for his wife to take his snapshot. For a battling saltbanker it was a comedown to be moored in that stagnant inlet of the Chicago River for a whole summer, but it was far better than going hungry.

Two years later *Bluenose* was again spruced up for exhibition—this time not for a crowd of corn-growing Americans but for the King and Queen of England, who were celebrating the twenty-fifth anniversary of their reign in April, 1935.

Bluenose was almost a dowager herself by that time. Almost fifteen years had passed since the first dories, swinging over the rails to nest upon her deck, had scarred her blue-black sides. She had swollen considerably with the seawater in her timbers, and the grounding at Placentia Bay had hogged her a bit, but she was still the handsomest lady at the royal review.

When word came to Angus that the King himself planned to come aboard, he asked, "Wit' de missus?" and hurriedly sent ashore for a bottle of King George whiskey so that he could offer His Majesty a drink. At the last moment other obligations crowded in upon King George, and instead of going over himself he invited Walters to visit with him on the royal yacht. The King embarrassed his sons by referring to *Bluenose* as a herring fisher, but Angus took no offense, realizing that the King had too great a variety of ships to think about, to keep proper track of each of them.

All the same, it was a signal moment in a long life of gallant service. *Bluenose,* dressed in a glistening new suit of sails, had crossed the Atlantic Ocean as the representative of a vast and beautiful country whose greatness was still to be discovered. Canada, silent under her mantle of snow, had sent forth her finest product to speak in her name, and no one who watched *Bluenose*

85

sailing into Plymouth with her wings to the wind could have failed to hear her message.

On her return voyage, a hundred and fifty miles off the English coast, *Bluenose* was caught in a furious storm. Walters ordered the crew to take down all her sails except the jumbo and the storm sail, but she was taking a terrific beating from the sea. She was leaking "300 strokes to the hour" and foundering heavily aft from all the water in her stern. At the height of the storm, one of the two other men on deck shouted to Angus to "cut out her spars!"

"There'll be no spars cut out of the *Bluenose!*" he shouted back. Moments later the vessel was struck broadside by the biggest sea ever. *"Bluenose* keeled over on her beam-ends. Her belowdecks flooded with tons of water. Both boats were smashed; the deckhouse engine box, the foreboom and the mainboom jaws were smashed; her galley was uprooted and her port bulwarks vanished. She stayed under—masts and all—for a full five minutes. I was sure she was a goner. No other wooden vessel could have survived such a blow without splintering into smithereens."

Then with a great shudder, the queen shook herself free of the heaving waters and righted herself. But the pounding had opened her seams aft. Walters summoned all hands and his passengers as well. They ripped up the flooring and, crawling about in the blackness of her bilge, shifted the pig-iron ballast forward to offset the weight of the tons of water dragging down her after end. Furious efforts on the hand pumps finally balanced the water going out with the water coming in, and she was able to limp back to Plymouth, a full week after she had sailed away with all flags flying. Angus denied that he was surprised at her capacity for taking the very worst punishment the savage seas could deliver. "Except for four hours, she ran with her mains'l furled the whole time," he said.

Chapter Ten

The year 1935 was a triumphal one for *Bluenose,* but her crew could not live on glory. Before the summer was over she was back on the Banks, filling her hold with salt cod and worrying about the future. There was no doubt about it: Changes were on their way. She simply could not afford to stay home six months of the year. Like the rest of the working fleet she would have to refit for winter fishing.

The idea was hard to swallow, but the following year even the champion had to face the facts. Engines were installed in her hull, and a narrow black smokestack made its appearance just fore of her cabin. It was better than tying up, but to Angus it must have felt like sailing with one arm in a sling. The engines helped speed up the trip, but they could not cure the sickness that was ailing the salt-fish industry. Everyone, from cabinet ministers down to salt shovelers, was complaining about hard times, but some men were hurting in their bank accounts and some men were hurting in their bellies. Finally talk of unions began even in Nova Scotia. The fishermen asked the fish dealers for a quarter-of-a-cent-per-pound raise in the price of fish, but the fish dealers said no.

There had never been a revolt in the whole history of the town of Lunenburg, but the tart little skipper of *Bluenose,* who hadn't winced at the toughest weather, was not going to stand by mute and helpless just because it was the tradition of the town to "put up and shut up." Angus talked to the other skippers about backing up the demands of the fishermen. They were willing, but, they asked, how about the steam trawlers? Trawlers had the lion's share of the market now. Unless they joined, the schoonermen would just be committing suicide to fight the dealers alone.

"Then we'll get the trawlers to go out as well," he replied.

Walters was elected president of the organization which tied up Lunenburg tighter than a towline. The fish dealers were furious. "That Angus! Stirring up the town! Setting neighbor against neighbor! Aren't we all in this thing together? He's just too independent! Who does he think he is, anyway?" But the strike went on.

Meanwhile not a single cod swung in the scales, not a single trawl line worked its way down to the ocean's floor. The town was split into factions by the battle, and there were many who put the main blame on Angus. By and large his fellow fishermen were not impressed by their wealthier critics. "Oh, him," said one of them of a town father, *"he's got eyes like a dead haddock!"*

It was a hard fight, piling unemployment on top of poverty, but finally the fishermen won. Along with the rest of the old-timers, Angus took *Bluenose* back to the Banks, but even with the quarter-of-a-cent-per-pound increase, it was hard going. Some of the older vessels which tied up during the strike never did get back into fishing. No one had the money to put them into working shape. Water-logged and raunchy, some were sold to Newfoundlanders who, being even poorer than the Nova Scotians, sailed them until they sank. A few vessels were sold to work in the coastal freighting trade in the West Indies.

Bluenose herself was begining to look more like a scullery maid than a queen. All sorts of gear wanted paint or replacement, and $7200 was still owing on the engines which had been installed in 1936. She enjoyed the honor of having her likeness appear on every ten-cent piece minted by the Canadian Government. Her portrait had been carved in relief by a Toronto sculptor named Emanuel Hahn, but the honor would not buy a new suit of sails or even pay off the interest on her debt.

In the spring of 1938 a newspaperman from the *Halifax Herald* came down to Lunenburg to talk racing again with Angus. "You don't know what you're talkin' about, Mr. Curry," said Walters. "Why, it would take near $10,000 to put the *Bluenose* into shape for a race. She took a terrible beating that time off the English coast. I'm not takin' her out to insult her, you know. Why, she's eighteen years old! She needs a lot of work!"

"Think she's too old to win?" Curry asked innocently. "Think she couldn't beat the *Thebaud* anymore?"

"Of *course* she'd beat the *Thebaud*! She did it when *Thebaud* was fresh off the stocks, and she'd do it now. But I wouldn't drag a record like hers in the dirt by taking her to any race unprepared. What's the sense in talkin' about it? Where am I goin' to find $10,000? You tell me that!"

"Suppose the Americans were to put up the money?"

"The *Americans*? Do you take me for a fool, after all the fights I've had with the Americans and their bloody committees?"

"How about if they paid you in advance?"

"Seein's believin' " countered Walters.

When all the talk was over it boiled down to the promise of $11,000—$1000 to come from the Canadian Government, and $8000 from the American committee, half of that to be paid in advance. The balance would be prize money, just in case *Bluenose* should win again.

It was a lot of money to dangle in front of *Bluenose*'s bowsprit, enough to give the old vessel a new lease on life. But Walters dreaded the prospect of the endless quarreling he knew would be part and parcel of a race with the Americans. He was outraged by the fact that the people of his own town, of his own province, would not put up a thin Canadian dime to defray the cost of preparing *Bluenose* for the race, that he would have to make all necessary loans on his personal responsibility—and he a poor man in a rich town. *Bluenose* deserved the help even if she hadn't been a champion. She'd paid back her investors 151 percent on every dollar they'd put into her. Why couldn't Lunenburgers see that this was something worth doing—for their country if for nothing else?

Lunenburg did have one citizen, a wealthy sportsman named R. C. S. Kaulbach, who felt strongly enough about *Bluenose* to offer to match, dollar for dollar, any amount of money the town would raise. To save all embarrassment, he opened a special account in a Lunenburg bank, in which people could deposit as much or as little as they liked, even if it was only a twenty-five-cent piece. Kaulbach himself was prepared to put up thousands. After six weeks had passed, it was Kaulbach who felt embarrassed. His fellow townsmen had not contributed a penny. He went back to the bank and closed the account.

The town pleaded poverty, but there must have been a few, at least, who rather enjoyed the sight of their old nettle-tongued enemy dangling from a fishhook.

Good sense told Angus that the race was just an excuse for a lot of gambling men to have a big fling. Intuition told him that this might be the very last time anyone would sail in a Fishermen's International Competition, and the very last chance to save his vessel from humiliating ruin. If she won, perhaps Canadians would be proud enough and grateful enough to provide her with an honorable retirement, to preserve her so that future generations could see with their own eyes the stuff that Canada was made of. That was the only hope which lay underneath all of Angus's sarcasm. It was the only prize he coveted.

Long after the man from the *Halifax Herald* had departed, Angus paced *Bluenose*'s broad deck, trying to make up his mind. His gaze traveled upward, along the whole immense length of her mainmast, and lost itself among the stars. He heard the music of the sea lapping at the sides of his beloved vessel, felt the soundness of her deck beneath his feet. "It's a gamble. . . . What do you say, old girl?" he asked her.

Bluenose must have nodded, for instead of making her fourth trip to the Banks that season, she slid discreetly into the outfitters' wharf.

She looked terrific that crisp October day in 1938, sailing out of Lunenburg for the run to Gloucester. She was beautiful in the way that a pair of capable hands are beautiful and tell more about a person, sometimes, than a face. Inspired with their sense of mission, her crew sprang to her captain's orders. When there was nothing more to do but crowd the rail and watch the sea rush past, one man after another strolled aft, hoping to chat with Angus. But he was enveloped in a private conversation.

"Hush up," he would say to those who wanted to pass the time of day. "The old girl's talkin' to herself. I gotta listen to what she's sayin'!" Speak to him she did, in every creak and mutter of her working timbers, in every hammerblow of her prow against the glistening sea, in every surge of rope and canvas against the wind. In his perfect control, perfect oneness with his vessel, he knew a freedom that was also perfect. It was a feeling many men dream of but few experience.

Angus knew long before he set out for Gloucester that five races had been scheduled for this series. He thought it was a waste of time. "If *Thebaud* can't beat *Bluenose* in three races, she certainly won't be able to do it in five." But the two additional races were a small grievance, compared to the main issue: The $4000 promised by the Americans had never arrived in Lunenburg. When Angus demanded the money that was coming to him, he was met with a grudging check for half that sum, instead, and the remainder was promised for later.

Nothing stung like being on the receiving end of an opponent's niggardly handout. No doubt the Americans felt that they were being quite generous to underwrite the cost of putting their rival into racing trim. Americans never seem to have learned how to give money away without enraging the people they give it to, and this occasion was no exception. On Walters's side, there was good reason for indignation. It wasn't his fault that he wasn't rich. He hadn't asked for any handouts. It was the Americans who had pressed the race upon *him*, and he had only taken them at their word.

By the time the race was to begin, the atmosphere was supercharged with anger on both sides. Everything seemed to be off on the wrong foot. Ben Pine had taken the wheel of *Thebaud* again, but even Ben was looking poorly. In the opening race *Bluenose* was a full three minutes late in crossing the starting line, and in an echo of the very first race with *Elsie*, she lost her fore-topmast before she reached the finish. *Thebaud* won by nearly as much as her initial lead.

The Americans cheered themselves hoarse. It must have been clear to many that this might be the last chance they would have to try to take the cup away from the dour little Canadian in the big sweet boat who had dared to beat them time and time again, and they made the most of it.

In the second race, held on October 13, *Bluenose* was first over the starting line and first at the finish by a fat twelve-minute margin. The score for the series stood at one to one.

There followed days of fog and calm, and in the heat of all the talk an American with a very sharp eye noted that *Bluenose* had swollen around the waist, that her waterline was over the maximum length of 112 feet provided for in the racing regulations. Her measurements were taken and sure enough, middle-aged spread had added fully two feet to her girth. Lacking a girdle to fit a ship, her crew set about removing some of her ballast so that she would ride higher and shorter on the water. The adjustment boomeranged against the Americans, for with the weight removed, she handled sprightlier than ever.

Meanwhile, Ben Pine fell ill and the wheel of *Thebaud* was turned over to her regular skipper, Capt. Cecil Moulton. *Bluenose* won the third race by six minutes. But *Thebaud* won the fourth race by two. The backstay on *Bluenose* had snapped, and two men on her masthead were in great danger from the flailing cable. Walters ordered the jib topsail doused, but despite frantic efforts by her crew, *Bluenose* could not make up the time lost in altering her sail. The series stood two to two.

The fifth and final race was to be held on October 26. Angus knew full well when he stepped aboard *Bluenose* that day that this was to be no ordinary race. Much, much more was being fought out over this racing course than met the eye. At stake was a hundred-and-fifty-year-old contest between Canada and her big, boisterous, overbearing neighbor for the recognition of the rights of smaller, less powerful nations. Lawyers and politicians had fought the battle with treaties and tariffs and in legal limitations on fishing rights. Shipwrights had fought it in design, in inventiveness, in craftsmanship. Fish dealers had fought it in markets and price wars, in production methods; and fishermen and skippers had fought it with hard work and increased speed.

Nearly always the States had won. There was money in the States, and maneuverability, and efficiency, and know-how, a spirit of get-up-and-go. But far too often, "Let's get the job done!" was followed by an unspoken ". . . and the devil with anyone who gets in the way!" Canada's feelings toward the United States were diplomatically cordial, but the resentment of Canadians toward their rich cousins to the south ran fathoms deeper than could be measured by any sounding lead.

Maybe Angus felt all that when he took the smooth metal wheel of his vessel in his calloused hands that morning. Or maybe his head was so full of practical everyday thoughts of what had to be done to win the race that he didn't stop long enough to think those larger thoughts. Some small part of *Bluenose*'s superstructure had given way in nearly every race. What would snap in this one? Could his vessel take the strain? How hard dared he push her? Could he possibly win? Could he possibly *lose?* His whole being, everything he had ever wanted to prove in his lifetime, was at stake.

The starting gun sounded, and *Thebaud* and *Bluenose* sprang across the line like a pair of wild winged horses.

"Come on, you long black witch!" cried Angus as his beloved burned across the water. As they rounded the last marker, he dropped to his knees to plead, "One more time, old girl, just one more time!"

Bluenose gave him everything he asked for, and more. In spite of a broken block on the very last leg of the race, she'd logged an average speed of 14.15 knots, the *fastest pace ever recorded over a fixed course by a canvased vessel in the history of sailing!* She crossed the line three minutes ahead of America's best.

For a few moments an awed crowd paid a silent tribute to the aged queen. And then a roar went up that filled the sky. *Bluenose* had fought for Canada with sheer spirit, and sheer spirit had won the race. She took the applause simply, with a dowager's unassuming modesty. It was her finest hour, her greatest triumph.

Chapter Eleven

Angus Walters and *Bluenose* had heard the acclaim of an ador-
ing public ring in their ears for the last time. What followed was
a disgrace both to Americans and to Canadians. The American
committee staged a party for the winning crew, but they claimed
they couldn't find the trophy until the ritual banquet was over,
and then they handed it to Angus wrapped in old newspapers.
Worse still, the committee never paid him all they had promised, and the partial payment he finally received was obtained
only after he had brought a lawyer into the case.

Back in Lunenburg a movement was organized to launch
a Canada-wide campaign to preserve *Bluenose* as a national treasure. Subscriptions of a dollar apiece would be sold throughout
the country. But the movement got lost in endless discussion. No
one wanted to assume enough responsibility to guarantee that it
would work, and without such guarantee, those who might have
given were not willing to risk their money. Besides all that, another war was brewing on the horizon.

Angus was fifty-seven years old in 1939, and he had been
doing battle, both on the Banks and off, for nearly all that time.
"How long're you gonna stick with fishin'?" people asked him.
He could stick with fishing as long as there were fish, or he could
"swallow the anchor," a feat which is every bit as hard and pain-
ful as it sounds for a saltwater man. Walters had too much pride
to hang onto old victories. Besides, he'd proved his point.

People had been saying for a long time that Lunenburg
needed a modern pasteurizing plant to process all the milk that

was produced in the area. When it came to drama, cows were no match for canvas, but Angus had to find some sort of work he could keep on doing for the rest of his life. He decided to go into the dairy business, but he put his barn as close to the harbor as he could get it without wetting his doorstep.

Another skipper took the helm of *Bluenose,* and then a second replacement, but she never performed for either of them the way she had for Angus. Besides, crewmen and fishermen

were getting scarcer all the time. Many young Nova Scotians entered military service, and even Newfoundlanders, who would cross the Atlantic on a log, were getting wary of sailing about in wooden vessels with another war at hand. *Bluenose* made a few trips, but they netted hardly enough to pay her fishermen. By the end of the year she tied up at the wharf and sat with her hands in her lap like some old auntie, fondly remembered but rarely visited.

Canada, with England, made her official entry into World War II in 1939, and very soon thereafter the war became the greatest death-dealing machine ever created on earth, consuming more than fifty million lives before it ceased. In its midst very few people gave any thought to salt fishing, and among the few who did, there were none who believed that the industry would ever make a comeback, not even Angus.

In spite of all the money spent in getting *Bluenose* into racing shape, the company which had installed the engines in her hull, back in 1936, had still not been paid. Her shareholders were not willing to put any more money into her, for she had no future as a fishing boat. There wasn't a wooden vessel afloat which had. Sentiment was one thing, but these were terrible times. Millions of people were fighting and dying, and an obsolete old fishing vessel just didn't seem very important.

Angus was bitter about it. "They just couldn't see any personal profit in it," he said. "All the honor *Bluenose* brought to Canada, brought to the town, all the money the fishermen put in their pockets . . . why, they all got rich off the fishing fleet. They could've fixed her up so's people could understand the sort of life those men lived, the work they done, what kind of character it took to build a champion. . . ."

But the money could not be raised. *Bluenose* was to be put up on the auction block. The date was set, the bids were sealed, and Angus spent one sleepless night after another eating his heart out over the indifference of mortal men. The morning of the auction, he went to the home of the president of a Lunenburg bank. It was a Saturday, and all the banks were closed. But this particular president, confronted by this particular man, decided that some things were more important than regular banking hours. He opened up the bank and took Angus's signature on a loan for $7200. When the auctioneer raised his hammer to ask, "What am I bid?" Angus put not only his life savings but his whole financial future on the table, to become the sole owner of an aging and unprofitable workhorse whose only claim upon his affection and loyalty was that she had given him the best years of his life.

It was a noble gesture, but it was only a delaying action. Only a rich man could have afforded to keep a vessel idle year in and year out. When at last the West Indian Trading Company offered to buy her, the old man couldn't quite say "Yes," but he nodded his head.

During the depression it often happened that a husband and wife who had lived side by side for half a century had to part from each other because none of their grown children had room enough or money enough to keep them both. How do people say good-bye when the parts of their lives that touched have grown together like the twin trunks of a forked tree? How does one face the certain knowledge that the dear familiar face will disappear forever, once the train departs from the station? Does one say, "Good-bye, old friend. . . . It's been good to know you"?

It was a sad, gray day in March, 1940. Down in Lunenburg harbor, Angus asked the men who stood about on *Bluenose*'s wharf to leave him alone for a little while. He had to say good-bye, and he had to do it all by himself. No one but him would unwind the heavy rope which held *Bluenose* to her mooring. No one but him would watch while she slipped away for the last time into the mist.

Everyone understood. Together, *Bluenose* and Angus Walters had performed miracles. Each of them had created greatness in the life of the other. Apart, they would be just another old man and just another old fishing boat.

Chapter Twelve

Far too many young Canadians were killed in the course of World War II for people to linger long over smaller sorrows. For the men who had sailed in her, *Bluenose* was a vanished home, the symbol of youth and daring, of a life-style that would never be duplicated. For Angus Walters, she left an aching void where his heart used to be.

For four long, dreary years, *Bluenose* plied the submarine-free waters of the West Indies, chugging along with sails or without, her great hold filled with molasses, sugar, bananas, tobacco. While she sailed her modest way about the islands, her old rival, *Gertrude L. Thebaud,* patrolled the eastern coast of her country, serving as the honored flagship of the U. S. Coast Guard's Corsair fleet.

Now and again someone would recognize the old queen from her lines, would comment on the three interlocking gold rings on her sternplate that marked her as a Lunenburger, and there would be a flurry of talk. But her days of glory were over. Even the numbers by which her fantastic speed was reported around the world grew inaccurate and her story, worn bare by frequent repetition, stale. "Yeah, she was some fast boat," people would say, and go on to more important matters.

A month after the agony of World War II was finally ended, *Gertrude Thebaud* left Gloucester for the last time, for she, too, had finally been sold to work in the Central and South American freighting trade. If the two vessels ever met, no one has reported the encounter, but it would have been the occasion for many a tearful "remember when."

On January 28, 1946, less than a year after the war was over, word flashed over the teletypes that *Bluenose* had struck a reef off the coast of Haiti. Not long before she was born, it had taken two weeks for news of the signing of the Treaty of Versailles to get from Paris to Halifax. Twenty-seven years later word of *Bluenose*'s catastrophe reached Lunenburg quickly enough for Angus to plead with the Canadian Government to send a rescue mission down to Haiti to tow her off the rocks. Her crew had escaped, but they'd returned the next day and had taken out her engines.

Angus wanted to fly down to Haiti himself to direct a salvage operation, but reports about the vessel's position and condition were fuzzy and contradictory, some saying that she was breaking up, others that she was slipping into deep water, still others that she had already vanished completely. The rescue effort got lost somewhere among the many layers of government authority and before decisive action was taken, the moment for action had passed, for she was gone. No one ever brought the whole story home to Lunenburg. No one ever turned up so much as a splinter of the wreckage. But the town talked about it, off and on, for years and years and years.

Less than two years later, *Thebaud* went down off the northern coast of Venezuela. The era of magnificent wooden fishing vessels had come at last to a close.

⚓

Up in Lunenburg, things were changing. Time itself began to move more and more slowly. The center of the fishing industry moved away from the Nova Scotian coast. Lunenburg harbor, where two hundred bowsprits had once tuned in on the gossip of the town, lay empty and silent. They were building bigger and bigger boats down in the States, not only the old-fashioned beam trawlers which stretched an arm over their side to sweep tens of thousands of pounds of fish into a net with a single motion, but also stern trawlers which payed out the line on gigantic power-driven winches from the stern. Salt fishing was taken over by

Newfoundlanders and Norwegians and, still later, by Russians who sent as many vessels to the Banks as the Americans. More and more of the freezing and processing of the fish was being done aboard the vessels themselves, and everything but the glint on the fish scales was converted to some commercial purpose.

Scarcely noticed at first was the fact that with every mouthful the new fishermen took from the sea, they were removing from the Banks some of the precious surface which nourished the fish, till the great schools which had once made those waters hard for a small boat to navigate because of the sheer density of fish life began to thin out and eventually disappear. Over a fifty-year period, cod catches on the Banks declined to one fifth of what they had been at the beginning of the century, both in spite of and because of the improved technology. At the present time two billion pounds of cod are being caught each year off the coast of Iceland, ten times the amount of fish that once came from the Grand Banks, but no one knows whether the cod have been moving steadily northward or if they were always there and are only now being caught. But reason says that it will be only a matter of time before man and his improved machinery exhaust and despoil this great Icelandic abundance as well.

Yet in spite of all these changes, life in Lunenburg went on. Though most of the young men left the town to find work other than fishing, the old-timers still built small boats for the inshore fisheries, sometimes catching just enough to keep the family fed and healthy. Though a big fish-processing plant was built late in the fifties, the older folks resigned themselves to the knowledge that Lunenburg would never again be a bustling center of world commerce, and they settled down to enjoy their tranquillity.

While Lunenburg dozed or paused in the sun to have its picture taken by "rusticating American tourists," the rest of the American continent got caught up in a wild postwar pursuit of comfort, prosperity, and "progress." The more things people acquired, the more tired and bored they became. Vacation-taking became hard work too. People whose parents had lived a lifetime without ever pausing in their work except to attend a wedding or a funeral began a frantic search for "places to go." To more and more people, Nova Scotia became a romantic faraway place in which to escape from the dull routine and turmoil of the big city for two precious weeks of "living." Nova Scotians who had learned so much about catching lobsters and codfish now went about finding ways of catching tourists.

Then a very strange thing happened. From the very opposite end of the continent an unfamiliar voice was heard in Lunenburg. It came from Hollywood, California. It was not only that Hollywood was as far to the southwest of the American continent as Lunenburg was to its northeast. It was also that if you were to turn Lunenburg inside out, or stand it on its head, you would get Hollywood, and vice versa. Hollywood was as rich and glamorous as Lunenburg was poor and plain. For all of Lunenburg's hardy self-reliance, Hollywood was a world of favors, where fortunes turned on a smile, and women swam in pools of champagne. Hollywood, dream-maker to the world, bubble-blower, magician, ballyhooer par excellence, personified all the corruption and phonyness and show-off fictions—multiplied a million times over—that Lunenburg loathed about Yankees. What would Hollywood want with Lunenburg?

As it turned out, she wanted shipbuilders.

Metro-Goldwyn-Mayer was going to do a film called *Mutiny on the Bounty*, starring Marlon Brando, and they needed to have a replica of the *Bounty* built. Lunenburg had the shipyards, Lunenburg had the shipwrights, and Lunenburg got the contract. Smith & Rhuland hadn't built many square-riggers, but they'd built *Bluenose*, and they would produce a solid, substantial vessel, no doubt about it.

Lunenburg could overlook the cigar-smoking executives who would take in the town with a single glance and say, with a deprecating nod, "Nice place you got here. . . ."

While the *Bounty* was being built, many people came to look and before Lunenburg fully awoke to the fact, the shipyard had become a major tourist attraction.

Building the *Bounty* was only part of the task. People had to be found who could sail her as well. There were only a handful of men left in the world who knew how to handle sail well enough to undertake the job, but Nova Scotia had one of the best among her citizens. He was Capt. Ellsworth T. Coggins, of

Dartmouth. Coggins took the job, hired and trained a crew of Nova Scotian boys, and took the *Bounty* to Tahiti, then all around the world to advertise the film.

From the very first day the *Bounty* began to take shape Lunenburg people sighed and said, "If only it were the *Bluenose!*" Everyone in the town said it. Twenty years of talk had worn all the anger off the old factions, and men didn't want to go to their graves bearing grudges. Many of the tourists who came to Lunenburg were surprised and disappointed to learn that *Bluenose* wasn't there anymore. Even the newspapers began to say that it was a shame and a pity that Canadians had not acted to preserve the great vessel when there had still been time. But if Lunenburg could build a replica of the *Bounty* for "the Americans," why couldn't it also build an exact replica of *Bluenose* for "the Canadians"? Someone went over to see Bill Roue, now in his eighties, and found that he still had all the plans for *Bluenose* in his office—dusty, maybe, but still serviceable.

Angus was against the idea. It had taken twenty years for his hurt to heal, and he couldn't see any point in reopening old wounds. What was past was past. Suppose they did start a replica and then didn't raise enough money to finish her or keep her? Suppose they turned her into something awful and cheap, like a motel or a bar, and put up ugly neon signs all over the town saying, "This way to ye olde *Bluenose*"? He knew from his own experience how it wearied his spirit to be the town's leading "character," to be trotted out on state occasions to make a little speech full of colorful recollections, talking to newspaper people who didn't know a mast from a fishing pole.

But then another small miracle took place.

A Halifax brewery, the company which manufactured "Schooner Beer," decided to put up the major part of the money to build an exact replica of *Bluenose*. All the members of the Oland family, which owned the brewery, were sailing enthusiasts. They were not only good businessmen but men with enough public spirit to be keenly aware of Canada's need for symbols of her nationhood.

Down at Smith & Rhuland's yard, everything came back to life again. The air resounded to the whine of saws and the *clip-clip* of adzes. Two of the same men who had built *Bluenose I* went to work on *Bluenose II* more than forty years later. If Angus Walters had ever wanted for honors from his fellow countrymen, the Oland family made up for all of it. At the keel-laying ceremony in February, 1963, when Angus struck the symbolic spike which his predecessor, the Governor-General of Canada, had missed in 1921, "there wasn't a dry eye in the house." When *Bluenose II* was launched in July, the Olands threw the biggest party ever seen in Lunenburg. There was a dory loaded with Schooner Beer, and enough fish chowder to feed hundreds and hundreds of guests.

Bluenose II is equipped with powerful engines, radar, sonar, and all the most modern devices to make her safer and more comfortable than her namesake. The only smell of fish comes now from her well-appointed galley. Her cabins are walnut-lined staterooms, her dining saloon is covered with wall-to-wall carpeting, and there isn't a Nova Scotian fisherman alive who'd take his boots off in the elegance of her hold. She spends her summers visiting about in the Maritime Provinces, and her winters working on charter in the West Indies. Her owners say she will never race, but unofficially she's logged twenty knots in a fair "breeze o' wind."

During Expo '67 year in Montreal, *Bluenose II* acted as the official host ship for the Canadian Government, welcoming and entertaining the crews of hundreds of ships which visited at Cité du Havre. Over one million people walked about her deck, marveling at the intricate web of line and steel that made up her rigging, posing at her wheel to have their pictures taken, just as people had done on *Bluenose I* at the Chicago world's fair.

Angus was aboard on her maiden voyage, when her owners took her down to the West Indies for the very first time. They ran into a hurricane just off the Jersey coast, and everyone felt a lot more confident about getting through the storm, knowing he was aboard. He was well into his eighties when he held the wheel of *Bluenose II* in his gnarled old hands and felt the wind surging against her canvas. He wrinkled his nose a bit, cocked his head to one side as if he were listening for a long-lost voice, and said to the men gathered by his side, "She's a wery fine wessel!"

Epilogue

A short time after Lunenburg celebrated the reappearance of *Bluenose*'s celebrated profile in her harbor, people in the town began to look about to see what else they might do to preserve the memory of a glorious past. The only saltbanker left was a half-submerged vessel named *Theresa B. Connor*, sagging on the outermost fringe of Lunenburg harbor. Ragged with seaweed, rust, and peeling paint, she had been abandoned in 1961, when her skipper could no longer assemble a crew to take her fishing. He had sailed her up to Newfoundland, but not even the Newfoundlanders were willing to go out fishing in a dory anymore.

A few old-timers went out to have a look at *Connor*. It was eerie poking around in the dimness of her hull, sniffing the old smells of salt and tar and fish and bilge, knocking old knuckles against blackened timbers. "Bald-headed old scow," someone called her, wiping away a tear. "She's still solid."

The town did what Angus said long ago they ought to do. They hauled her out of the drink, painted her inside and out, and anchored her at the foot of the old town. Everyone in Lunenburg rummaged through his attic for old oilskins, for sea charts, logs, leads, nameplates, lanterns, trawl buckets. When they got *Connor* up into the light they found a carefully lettered copy of the Ten Commandments tacked up over the captain's charts. God seemed to have a lot to do with sailing then. Angus Walters turned over the four-foot international fishermen's
106

trophy to *Connor*, for she had become the town's museum, the long-postponed fulfillment of Lunenburg's obligation to a great tradition.

So as things turned out, Angus got his wish after all. The fishermen had their memorial, and *Bluenose* had a daughter who was every bit as beautiful as her mother had been—and free, besides, to sail the seas.

As for the rivalry between Canada and the States, the outcome was as ironic as any human drama could be. For Canada might never have got around to building another *Bluenose*, had it not been for Hollywood. The very qualities in American life which had so exasperated the Nova Scotians during the days of the schooner races—the extravagance, the exaggeration, the fantasy of which Hollywood is the final expression—were the very means by which Nova Scotia was moved to reclaim some of the heritage which had almost slipped from her hands.

Old-time fishermen like Russell Tanner said the old life was a terrible life, that people had more sense nowadays than to try to make a living by dory fishing. Captain Albert Spindler, who made schooner models in his spare time, looked back on seventy years at sea and said he'd wasted his life. But for every old fisherman who added it all up and said, "Never again," there was another old fisherman who had only one wish, and that was to be able to do it all over again. Most of the time both old fishermen inhabited the same body. Fishing on the Grand Banks was the worst of life. It was also the best.

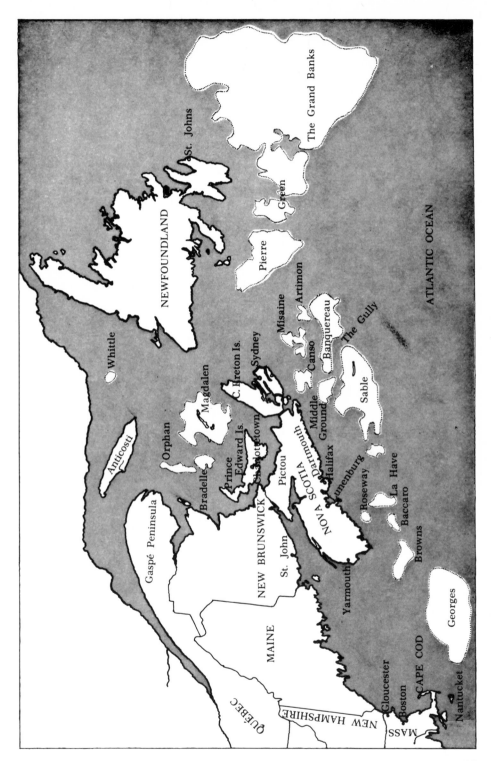

The Grand Banks

St. Johns

NEWFOUNDLAND

Green

Pierre

Artimon

Misaine

Banquereau

The Gully

ATLANTIC OCEAN

Whittle

Sydney

C. Breton Is.

Canso

Sable

Magdalen

Orphan

Prince Edward Is.

Charlotetown

Middle Ground

Anticosti

Bradelle

Pictou

Dartmouth

Halifax

Lunenburg

La Have

Roseway

Baccaro

Gaspé Peninsula

NEW BRUNSWICK

St. John

NOVA SCOTIA

Browns

Yarmouth

MAINE

Georges

QUÉBEC

NEW HAMPSHIRE

Gloucester

Boston

CAPE COD

MASS

Nantucket

Bibliography

Backman, Brian and Phil., *Bluenose*. Toronto, McClelland & Stewart, 1965.

Bird, Will R., *This Is Nova Scotia*. Toronto, Ryerson Press, 1951.

Carson, Rachel L., *The Sea Around Us*. New York, Oxford University Press, 1961.

Chase, Mary Ellen, *Fishing Fleets of New England*. Boston, Houghton, Mifflin, 1961.

Church, Albert C., *American Fisherman*. New York, W. W. Norton, 1940. Reprinted Toronto, George J. McLeod.

Gillespie, G. J., *Bluenose Skipper*. Fredericton, New Brunswick, Brunswick Press, 1955.

Innis, Harold A., *The Cod Fisheries: History of an International Economy*. Toronto, University of Toronto Press, 1954.

Kipling, Rudyard, *Captains Courageous*. Original printing London, 1895. Reprinted New York, Pyramid, 1966.

Marsh, James H., *The Fishermen of Lunenburg*. Toronto, Holt, Rinehart & Winston of Canada, 1968.

Merkel, Andrew, *Schooner Bluenose*. Toronto, Ryerson Press, 1949.

National Film Board of Canada, *The Sea Got in Your Blood*. Film documentary, David Millar, director.

Nicholson, F. W., *The Dory*. Halifax, Maritime Museum of Canada, Occasional Papers. 1960.

Pullen, Rear Adm. H. F. *Atlantic Schooners*. Fredericton, New Brunswick, Brunswick Press, 1967. (Atlantic Provinces Pavilion, Expo '67)

Thomas, Gordon W., *Fast & Able*. Gloucester, Mass., Historic Ships Associates, 1968.

Villiers, Capt. Alan, *The Quest of the Schooner Argos*. New York: Scribners, 1951.

Wallace, Frederick William, *Roving Fisherman*. Gardenvale, Quebec, The Canadian Fisherman, 1955.

Watt, John A., *A Brief Review of the Fisheries of Nova Scotia*. Halifax, Department of Trade and Industry, Province of Nova Scotia, 1963.

About the Author

Feenie Ziner was born in Brooklyn only a few days before *Bluenose* was launched in Lunenburg. She is a graduate of Brooklyn College and of the New York School of Social Work and was a psychiatric social worker before turning to writing.

Bluenose is her tenth published book. Five books are for young children. Two books for young adults tell the story of the Pilgrims. *Pilgrims & Plymouth Colony* presents the English side of the story, and *Dark Pilgrim,* published by Chilton, tells the same story from the Indian point of view.

In 1967, she published her first book for adults, *A Full House,* an autobiographical novel.

At the present time she is a lecturer in writing and contemporary literature at McGill University in the city of Montreal.

About the Artist

Zeke Ziner is a New Yorker whose special interests in fine arts have been sculpture and graphics. His work has been exhibited at the Museum of Modern Art, the Whitney Museum, the Art Institute of Chicago, the Los Angeles County Fair, and Library of Congress. He has had numerous one-man shows both here and abroad and has taught at the Institute of Design in Chicago and at the University of the City of New York. He worked in the advertising industry as a designer and art director both in New York and Chicago, and is presently director of marketing for the new town of Nuns' Island, under construction in the city of Montreal. Mr. and Mrs. Ziner have five children.